010
BORROWDALE GATES HOTEL

Grange In Borrowdale, Keswick, CA12 5UQ

017687 77204
www.borrowdale-gates.com

Colin Harrison proposed to his wife Joy at Surprise View, on the ancient packhorse route to Watendlath. As they gazed on the birds' eye panorama of Derwentwater and the surrounding mountains, they had no idea that one day the Borrowdale Gates Hotel, nestling on the other side of the lake under Catbells, would be theirs.

Growing out of lush gardens in the prettiest of Lakeland valleys, where Prince Charles has a bolt hole, the hotel's huge dining room windows confront magnificent Lakeland fells which are accessible from the doorstep. This former Victorian home of local benefactress Margaret Heathcote has undergone a major refurbishment by local craftsmen. Completed in spring, the upgrade lasted four years and includes a suite dedicated to a former local character, caveman and mountaineer Millican Dalton.

One outstanding aspect of the Borrowdale Gates is the sheer culinary pleasure of food sourced locally, where possible, and prepared by their dedicated and imaginative head chef Christopher Standhaven. With training from a Michelin Starred mentor, every meal is a symphony of delights, including Borrowdale trout and Herdwick lamb.

As a haven of peace and tranquillity in one of the most stunning locations in the entire UK, the Borrowdale Gates falls headlong into the category of hotels to visit before you die.

Colin and Joy have been supported by a team of highly professional and caring staff. Together they provide an enviable standard of service that ensures a steady return of clientele, including guests from California who have been returning to the Borrowdale Gates for 30 years. The combination of traditional values, attention to detail and keeping abreast of the times is the secret of Colin and Joy's success.

MUNCASTER CRAB & APPLE SALAD, SEARED SCALLOPS & PEA PUREE

SERVES 4

Inzolia (Italy)
Or Chardonnay, Philip Shaw (Australia)

Ingredients

Crab Salad

600g freshly picked crab
2 tbsp mayonnaise
5g chives (chopped)
1 lime (juice and zest of)
1 Granny Smith apple (peeled and grated)
6 king scallops (sliced into three)
a squeeze of lemon
salt and pepper

Pea Purée

200g garden peas
100ml double cream
5g fresh mint
salt and pepper

Apple Crisp (Optional)

1 Granny Smith apple
100g sugar
100ml water
1 lemon (juice)

Garnish

16 leaves red chicory endive
1 apple (*julienne*)
pea shoots

Method

For The Crab Salad

Place the crab, mayonnaise and chives in a bowl. Lightly mix together then add lime zest and juice. Peel and grate the apple, squeeze out the juice before adding so it doesn't make the crab too wet, then season to your taste with salt and pepper. Place in four individual small moulds and leave to set in the fridge for one hour.

> **Chef's Tip**
>
> If you can get hold of freshly picked crab, it will make the dish that extra special.

For The Pea Purée

Boil the peas in water for about two minutes then strain off and blitz in a food blender with the cream, fresh mint. Add salt and pepper. When smooth place in a squeezy bottle, ready to plate up later.

For The Apple Crisps (Optional)

Slice the apple as thinly as you can on a mandolin and then place sugar, water and lemon in a pan. Bring to a boil for three to four minutes then, take off heat and place your apple in the liquid until soft. Place on greaseproof paper in the oven on a low temperature until crisp.

For The Garnish

Peel the chicory into strips, cut the apple into little batons (*julienne*) and pick some nice pea shoots.

To Serve

Place the crab on the plate and arrange the chicory, *julienne* of apple and apple crisp next to the crab with a little pea shoot for garnish. Then, place some pea purée on the plate. Now cook the scallops in a hot frying pan until golden on one side, add a squeeze of lemon and a little salt and arrange on top of the crab. Drizzle the juices around the plate and over the scallops.

LAKE VIEW FARM FILLET OF BEEF, BUTTERNUT SQUASH, BRAISED OXTAIL & FOREST WILD MUSHROOMS

SERVES 4

🍷 *Shiraz & Cabernet, Willowglen (Australia),*
Or Rasteau Cotes du Rhone Villages, Domaine
Rasteau (France)

Ingredients

4 x 5 - 6oz fillets of beef
oil and butter for frying

Braised Oxtail
1kg oxtail (cut into pieces)
1 carrot
1 celery stick
1 onion
$^1/_2$ leek
2 bay leaves
1 sprig thyme
1 sprig rosemary
$^1/_2$ bottle red wine
1 ltr beef stock
salt and pepper

Red Wine Sauce
remaining stock from oxtail
200g trimmings of beef
250g diced vegetables (carrot, celery, onion and leek)
$^1/_2$ bottle red wine

Butternut Squash
1 butternut squash (for cubes and purée)
100g butter
1 lemon (juice)

Wild Mushrooms
200g mixed wild mushrooms
knob of butter
1 clove garlic
2 - 3 sprigs parsley (chopped)

Savoy Cabbage And Smoked Bacon
1 Savoy cabbage
4 slices smoked bacon
100g butter

Garnish
Chervil sprigs

Method

For The Oxtail
Quickly *seal* the oxtail in a pan then place in a deep tray or dish. Add the chopped vegetables, bay leaf, thyme, rosemary and the half bottle of red wine. Burn off the alcohol and then add the beef stock. Season and cover with tinfoil and cook for five hours in a slow oven at around 120 to 130°C, until the meat falls off the bone. When cooked, pick the oxtail off the bone and leave to cool. When cooled, roll into a cylinder in tinfoil and place in the fridge overnight to set.

> **Chef's Tip**
> Make sure the oxtail is braised until it falls off the bone, otherwise it will be very tough to eat.

For The Red Wine Sauce
Strain off the stock from the oxtail and remove any fat from the surface. Now sauté the vegetables and beef trimmings. When golden brown, add the red wine and the oxtail stock. Cook out for one hour, then turn up the heat and reduce by half. Strain off and, if it is not thick enough, reduce by half again. Season to taste and set aside.

For The Butternut Squash
Cut into four perfect squares and chargrill each side, then place in the oven at 170°C for ten minutes to cook through. Place the rest of the butternut squash into a pan and add a little water. Cook out until really soft and the water has evaporated, then add the butter, lemon juice and blitz until smooth.

For The Wild Mushrooms
Prepare the mushrooms and sauté with a little butter and garlic. Add the chopped parsley when golden brown.

For The Savoy Cabbage And Smoked Bacon
Slice the cabbage thinly and *blanch* in water and refresh in cold water. Thinly slice the bacon and fry with a little butter. When crispy, add the cabbage and cook slightly until soft.

To Serve
Preheat oven to 170°C. Colour the beef fillet in a frying pan with a little oil and butter then place in the oven for about eight to 12 minutes. Bring the oxtail out of the fridge and cut into four perfect pieces and panfry until soft, but not until it has lost its shape. Arrange the cabbage and bacon in the centre of the plate with the beef and wild mushrooms on top. Finish with the oxtail, chargrilled butternut squash and purée, red wine sauce and your picked chervil.

Castle Dairy expresses vibrant, contemporary fine dining in a characterful venue. The restaurant is located in Wildman Street, moments from the River Kent and Kendal town centre, the southern gateway to the Lake District.

COMPRESSED WATERMELON, GOLDEN BEETROOTS, CREAMED GOATS CURD

SERVES 4

 Chapel Down English Rose 2009, Tenterden Vineyards, Kent (England)

Ingredients

Compressed Watermelon

1 watermelon
150ml stock syrup (water 50g, sugar 50g)
5 star anise
1/2 cinnamon stick

Golden Beetroot

500g golden beetroot
75ml white wine vinegar
30g thyme
20g salt
8g white peppercorns
425ml water

Beetroot Carpaccio

1 large red beetroot
300ml red wine
50g soft brown sugar
10g pink peppercorns
2 star anise

Creamed Goats curd

100g goats curd
20ml Chardonnay vinegar
10ml whipping cream
salt
freshly ground white pepper

Vinaigrette

25g Dijon mustard
30g Chardonnay vinegar
150ml rapeseed oil

Method

For The Compressed Melon

Peel and slice the watermelon into one inch thick slices. Bring the stock syrup to a simmer, along with the star anise and cinnamon. Place each melon slice in a *vac-pac* bag with a little of the spiced stock syrup. *Vac-pac* on at the highest setting to compress the melon. Refrigerate for one hour then cut into one inch cubes.

For The Golden Beetroot

Place all ingredients in a large pan, bring to a boil and simmer until tender. Allow to cool in the liquid then peel the beetroot and cut into wedges.

For The Beetroot Carpaccio

Peel and thinly slice two thirds of the beetroot and use a cutter to punch out discs. Bring the wine, sugar and spices to a boil and add the discs. Simmer for two to three minutes and allow to cool in the liquor. *Julienne* the remaining beetroot for a garnish.

For The Creamed Curd

Beat the vinegar and cream into the goats curd until smooth, then season to taste. Place in a piping bag for later.

For The Vinaigrette

Whisk together mustard and vinegar, then slowly whisk in the oil until emulsified. Season to taste.

To Serve

Dress the beetroots and salad leaves with vinaigrette and plate as shown.

SEARED CANON OF LAMB, CONFIT BREAST, POTATO TERRINE, ENGLISH GARDEN PEAS, COURGETTES, WHITE ONION & GARLIC PUREE, LAMB JUS GRAS

SERVES 4

🍷 *Brouilly 2010, Henry Fessy, Crus Du Beaujolais, Burgundy (France)*

Ingredients

For The Meat

2 rack lamb
4g garlic powder
10g thyme
10g rosemary
1 lamb breast
10ml olive oil

Sauce

1ltr lamb stock (reduced)
4 banana shallots
4 carrots
1 head garlic
25g picked rosemary
40g rendered lamb fat
500ml red wine
1kg lamb bones (chopped)

Potato Terrine

500g Maris Piper potatoes
(peeled and thinly sliced)
150g *clarified butter*

Garlic Purée

3 head garlic (peeled)
2 white onions
1ltr milk
75ml double cream
100g butter

Garnish

2 courgettes
500g fresh garden peas
25g butter

Method

For The Meat

Remove the canon from the lamb rack and trim off sinew and fat. *Vac-pac* canons with olive oil, garlic powder, thyme and rosemary. Cook in a water bath at 53°C for one hour.

Season the lamb breast, roll in clingfilm, wrap in foil, then cook slowly at 130°C for four to five hours. Allow to cool, re-roll the breast and place in the fridge to set. Cut into portions when cold.

For The Sauce

Roast bones and vegetables at 180°C until golden brown. Pour off the excess fat (reserving it for later), then place into a saucepan. *Deglaze* the remains in the roasting tin with red wine and add to the pan. Reduce by three quarters, add the lamb stock and reduce to a sauce consistency. Pass through a fine sieve, then *monte* in a little of the lamb fat.

For The Potato Terrine

Mix potato and butter, season. Line a 4" x 8" terrine mould, or a small loaf tin, and layer up the potato. Cover with tinfoil and cook at 180°C for one and a half hours. Press the terrine and place in the refrigerator until cold. Cut into portions when it is set.

For The White Onion And Garlic Purée

Thinly slice the white onions and sweat them gently. Place the garlic in a pan with milk and bring to a boil. Repeat two more times and then continue to simmer the garlic until tender. Add the garlic and cream to the onions. Blend with remaining butter.

To Garnish

Turn the courgettes and cook. Double pod the peas and simmer in *emulsified* butter and water until tender.

To Serve

Fry the potato terrine and the lamb breasts until golden brown. Glaze the lamb breast with a little of the reduced lamb stock. Place them both in the oven to warm through. Remove the lamb canon from the water bath and sear in a very hot pan, rest for a moment then carve. Plate as shown.

Chef's Tip

If you don't have a water bath sear the lamb in a hot pan till golden brown on both sides, then into a hot oven for for five to eight minutes depending on size. Rest the lamb for the same amount of time as you have cooked it before carving.

WHIPPED VANILLA YOGHURT, WHITE BALSAMIC JELLY WITH STRAWBERRY MERINGUE, CONSOMME & SORBET

SERVES 4

Mouton Cadet Reserve Sauternes
(France)

Ingredients

Whipped Yoghurt

500g natural yoghurt
60g caster sugar
1 bourbon vanilla pod
35g Proespuma Cold Sosa

Sorbet

150ml water
100g caster sugar
50g glucose
500g strawberry purée
25ml vodka

Consommé

500g strawberries
50g caster sugar

Meringue

20g powdered egg whites
200g strawberry purée
100g caster sugar

White Balsamic Jelly

300ml white balsamic vinegar
150ml water
50g caster sugar
25g Vegetal Sosa (vegetable gelatine powder)

Garnish

8 English strawberries

Method

For The Whipped Yoghurt

With a small knife, remove the seeds of the vanilla pod and add to the rest of the ingredients. With a hand blender, mix all the ingredients until fully combined. Place in an espuma gun and charge with two Isi cream cartridges.

> **Chef's Tip**
>
> You can substitute a good natural set yoghurt for the recipe if you don't have an espuma gun, you will also not need the proespuma cold.

For The Sorbet

Place the water, sugar and glucose into a pan. Bring to a boil, making sure all the sugar has dissolved. Add the vodka and strawberry purée. Pass through a sieve. Chill overnight then churn in an ice cream machine until set.

For The Consommé

Vac-pac the strawberries and sugar together in a water bath for one hour at 85°C. Once cooked, leave to strain through muslin cloth overnight.

For The Meringue

Whisk the strawberry purée and powdered egg white together to stiff peaks. Gradually add the sugar and continue to whisk until the mix becomes glossy and shiny. Pipe onto Silpat mats and dehydrate at 80°C for 12 hours in a dehydrator, hot cupboard or a fan assisted oven.

For The White Balsamic Jelly

Place vinegar, sugar and water in a pan and bring to a boil. Slowly whisk in vegetal powder and heat to above 90°C to activate the setting agent. Pour into a mould and place in the fridge to set. Take the jelly out of the mould and cut into cubes.

To Serve

Cut the strawberries into quarters and plate.

030
CRAGWOOD
COUNTRY HOUSE HOTEL & RESTAURANT

Windermere, Cumbria, LA23 1LQ

015394 88177
www.cragwoodhotel.co.uk

Cragwood is a stunning country house hotel nestled on the shores of Lake Windermere. Set in its own secluded, 20-acre estate of beautiful Edwardian gardens, landscaped by Thomas Mawson, Cragwood has one of the most enviable locations in the Lake District.

Built in 1910, many of Cragwood's original features have been retained and lovingly restored, including beautiful wood panelling and magnificent fireplaces. Some of our rooms have gorgeous lake views so could there be a better place to watch the evening sun set over spectacular Coniston Old Man and the Langdale Pikes?

Under the creative and experienced direction of head chef Desmond Yare, dining at Cragwood is an experience not to be missed. Made with only the finest local and seasonal ingredients, you will discover a menu of freshly prepared and imaginative food, from simple classics to more contemporary combinations.

We believe in celebrating the region we live in and embracing all that is special and unique about the area. Food heroes like the local farmer, fisherman and butcher are the key to our home grown and local philosophy. We even have our very own resident chocolatier and speciality cake maker.

With two elegant and informal dining rooms overlooking the grounds and a garden terrace, Cragwood is a very special place to enjoy a meal with family or friends.

Made with only the finest local and seasonal ingredients, dining at Cragwood is an experience not to be missed. Head chef Desmond Yare has worked alongside such well known chefs as Raymond Blanc, Bruno Loubet and Marco Pierre White, bringing a creative flair to his imaginative menus.

HOMEMADE BRAWN, PICCALILLI & SAGE BEIGNET

SERVES 8 - 10

 Sauvignon Blanc, Casa Silva, Colchagua (Chile)

Ingredients

Homemade Brawn

1 cleaned pig's head (soaked for 24 hours)
4 carrots (peeled)
2 onions (chopped)
4 sticks celery
bouquet garni (this is a selection of fresh herbs tied together for flavour)
6 shallots (peeled and chopped)
1 tsp parsley (chopped)
1 tsp tarragon (chopped)

Piccalilli

175g cauliflower
175g green beans
175g cucumber
1 carrot (chopped)
175g silverskin onions
50ml white wine vinegar
100ml white wine
1 tsp mustard powder
$1/2$ tsp ground ginger
$1/2$ tsp ground turmeric
50g caster sugar
1 tbsp cornflour

Sage Beignet

50ml soda water
50ml ice water
115g plain flour
bunch sage leaves (picked)

Method

First Make The Piccalilli

Cut all vegetables into 1cm cubes. Cook vegetables, add vinegar and reduce then add wine and reduce. Add spices and sugar when vegetables are just tender. Add the cornflour mixed with a touch of water. Cook for a few seconds, remove from heat and place into a sterilised jar.

For The Brawn

In a stock pot, place the pig's head into cold water with the vegetables and bouquet garni. Cook for about three hours. Remove head from *liquor* when cold enough to handle. Chop the flesh, some of the fat, peel and chop the tongue. Season, then add shallots and herbs. Place into a clingfilm mould, moisten with some of the *liquor*, flatten and refrigerate for 12 hours. Remove from mould when serving.

For The Sage Beignet

Combine the soda water, ice water and flour to make the batter. Dip the sage leaves in and deep fry.

To Serve

Assemble a slice of brawn and sage beignet with a serving of piccalilli.

ASSIETTE OF DUCK, PAK CHOI, BLACK PUDDING, CELERIAC PUREE, MINI POMME FONDANT, HONEY & CRACKED BLACK PEPPER SAUCE

SERVES 2

Ninth Island Pinot Noir 2005
(Australia)

Ingredients

2 x 175g duck breasts

Confit

2 x 175g duck legs
1 sprig of thyme
1 garlic clove
500g goose fat

Bon Bon

75g plain flour
115g breadcrumbs
1 large egg

Pak Choi

1 pak choi (cut in half)
500ml chicken stock

Celeriac Purée

250g celeriac
300ml milk
1 garlic clove,
1 sprig thyme

Pomme Fondant

2 Uncle David's potatoes
1 clove garlic
1 sprig thyme
300/500g clarified butter

Black Pepper Sauce

500ml duck stock
1 tsp honey
1/4 tsp black pepper

carrots and asparagus (boiled until soft)

Method

For The Duck Breast

Cut into two and rub a little oil onto the skin, mixed with a pinch of salt and pepper. Place skin side down into a hot pan until golden brown, then turn over and put into the oven for five minutes at gas mark 7 (220°C). Rest for two minutes.

For The Duck Confit

Cook the duck legs in the goose fat with the thyme and garlic for three to five hours at gas mark 4 to 5 (180°C).

For The Duck Bon Bon

Using some of the duck leg confit, roll into two ball shapes. Coat in plain flour, egg wash and breadcrumbs. Deep fry until golden brown.

For The Pak Choi

Wash the pak choi then cut into halves. Slow cook in chicken stock for 20 to 30 minutes in an oven at gas mark 5 (180°C).

For The Celeriac Purée

Peel and cut the celeriac into cubes and cook in milk, thyme and garlic until soft. Drain milk off. Blitz and pass through a sieve.

For The Pomme Fondant

Peel and cut the potatoes with a cylindrical cutter. Cook in clarified butter, thyme and garlic for 20 to 30 minutes on a moderate heat until soft.

For The Black Pepper Sauce

Reduce duck stock, then add one teaspoon of honey. Add a quarter of a teaspoon of black pepper just before serving.

To Serve

Assemble dish as in picture or as desired. Serve with carrots and asparagus.

DARK CHOCOLATE MOUSSE WITH ITALIAN MERINGUE, WHITE CHOCOLATE ICE CREAM ON BLACK PEPPER TUILE

SERVES 8

 Muscat de Beaums-de-Venise, Bernardins, Rhone (France)

Ingredients

Mousse

200g bitter chocolate
300ml double cream

Pâté à Bomb

200ml water
300g caster sugar
5 egg yolks

Italian Meringue

120g caster sugar
1tsp glucose syrup
2 tbsp cold water
2 egg whites

Tuile Biscuit

115g caster sugar
115g butter
115g plain flour
83g egg white (whites of 2 eggs)
1 tsp black pepper

White Chocolate Ice Cream

500ml milk
500ml double cream
100g white chocolate (break into small pieces)
10 egg yolks
1 orange (zest)
300g caster sugar
200ml water

Method

For The Tuile

Cream the butter, sugar and add the flour, black pepper and egg whites, whisk until smooth. Leave to rest for ten minutes. Spread the tuile mix onto greaseproof paper and cook for five minutes at 180°C. Remove from greaseproof paper and shape as desired.

For The Mousse

Gently heat a pan of water, put the chocolate into a metal bowl over the pan whilst simmering, making sure the bowl is not touching the water. Stir the chocolate occasionally until melted.

Now make a *pâté à bomb*. Place the yolks into an electric mixing bowl on high speed, whisk until creamy. Boil the sugar and water to 121°C, then add it to the yolks. Mix slowly on a low speed whisk. Allow to cool. Add the melted chocolate mixture, stirring until the mixture is smooth and glossy. Whip the cream and fold in the mixture.

Finally, add the Italian meringue to make the mixture light and fluffy. It is made by boiling the sugar, glucose and water to 121°C. Then whisk the egg whites slowly and add the sugar syrup. Whisk until glossy.

Place the mixture into glasses or moulds and set in the fridge. The teardrop shape can be made by tempering 200g of dark chocolate. Once shaped you fill with mousse mixture and allow to set.

For The White Chocolate Ice Cream

Boil the milk and cream along with the orange zest in a pan and then add the chocolate until melted. Remove from the heat and allow to cool.

Boil both sugar and water in a saucepan to 121°C, then remove from heat and allow bubbles to subside. Use an electric whisk to whisk the egg yolks until smooth. Then, add the sugar syrup, pouring steadily whilst whisking until mixture is thick and pale and cooled to luke warm. Add this to the chocolate mixture and once cooled, churn in ice cream machine and freeze.

To Serve

Serve as in picture, or as desired. This dish would also look attractive served in glasses.

Chef's Tip
Glucose syrup is made from maize starch. This clear white liquid is also know as 'liquid glucose syrup'. It is available from most supermarkets in the baking section.

040
DALE LODGE HOTEL & TWEEDIES BAR

Red Bank Road, Grasmere, Cumbria, LA22 9SW

015394 35300
www.dalelodgehotel.co.uk

Dale Lodge Hotel is situated in the picturesque village of Grasmere, in the heart of the Lake District, between mountains and the lake with which the village shares its name.

The hotel has had a lot of work done to it over the years to transform the Georgian building from old fashioned to modern and stylish, where guests can enjoy a wide selection of award-winning real ales and wine, and the delicious food of head chef James Goodall.

James started his training in London at just 16, before going on to work in France, Spain and Australia. The experience and skills he gained there became invaluable and these influences can be seen in his work today. In 2002, he returned home to the Lake District and was head chef at The Log House Restaurant in Ambleside before opening Dale Lodge.

His full menu is available not just in the main Lodge Restaurant, but also in Tweedies Bar, so guests have the choice to dine in surroundings that suit their mood and the occasion.

Tweedies offers flagstone floors, log fires and most importantly seven guest ale pumps and a traditional scrumpy pump. The Lodge Restaurant is a more refined and elegant setting for a candlelit meal. Combined with the enormous beer garden, Dale Lodge is perfect for everything, from family gatherings to romantic getaways.

With a large range of award-winning real ales, extensive wine list and possibly the largest beer garden in The Lake District, Tweedies Bar is a wonderful place for a light lunch, family gathering or special occasion.

PANFRIED SCALLOPS & CAULIFLOWER PUREE WITH CUMBRIAN AIR DRIED HAM

SERVES 1

 Chardonnay Reserva, Vina Casa Silva (Chile)

Ingredients

For The Scallops

3 large fresh king scallops
(hand dived if possible)
1 tsp olive oil
$^1/_2$ lemon
pinch sea salt

Cauliflower Purée

1 cauliflower
300ml milk
50g butter

Deep Fried Sage

2 sprigs sage
100ml vegetable oil

Local Beech Air Dried Ham

1 piece of good quality air dried ham

Method

For The Crispy Air Dried Ham

Place the ham under the grill until nice and crispy, cover to cool.

For The Cauliflower Purée

Cut the stalk off the bottom of the cauliflower then cut the cauliflower into even pieces. Place in the milk and cook until soft. Purée the cauliflower with butter, whilst hot, using a stick blender or similar until it is smooth. Add salt and pepper to taste.

For The Deep Fried Sage

Pick the leaves off the stalks and deep fry at 300°C until crisp.

For The Scallops

Remove coral (orange coloured tail) and muscle (clear membrane around scallops) and pat the scallops dry. Heat a frying pan over a high heat. Add olive oil, place scallops in the pan and cook for 45 seconds on each side (or until coloured on both sides). Season with lemon juice and sea salt to taste.

> **Chef's Tip**
> Do not overcook the scallops, this will result in a bitter taste.

To Serve

Assemble as in picture.

ROAST RACK OF CUMBRIAN MUTTON, WITH PEA & MINT PUREE, MASH POTATO, BABY SUMMER VEGETABLES & BRAISED SHOULDER OF LAMB

SERVES 1

 Pinot Noir, Mud House, Central Otago (New Zealand)

Ingredients

1 rack of mutton (*French trimmed*)

Shoulder Of Lamb

1 lamb shoulder (you can get this from your local butchers)
3 sprigs fresh thyme
1/2 clove garlic (crushed)
5g sea salt
1 ltr chicken stock

Mash Potato

1 large King Edward potato
25g cream
25g butter
pinch salt and pepper

Pea And Mint Purée

200g peas
100ml chicken stock
25g butter
1 sprig mint

Summer Vegetables

2 baby carrots
2 baby turnips
2 baby fennel
5 broad beans
10g butter
salt and pepper

Sauce

25ml Madeira
150ml good quality lamb stock
2 shallots (chopped)
1 sprig rosemary
1 tsp olive oil

Method

For The Shoulder Of Lamb (best done the day before)

Grind together the thyme, garlic and sea salt in a pestle and mortar. Rub the mixture into the lamb shoulder. Marinade in fridge overnight.

Wash off the remaining mixture. Place the shoulder of lamb in a deep roasting tray. Cover with one litre of chicken stock and cook in a preheated oven at 150°C for six hours.

Remove from the oven and leave to cool. Using your fingers, shred the meat and season to taste. Layer clingfilm onto a flat surface area and spread the lamb evenly throughout the clingfilm. Roll into a sausage shape. Refrigerate for one hour.

Just before serving, slice off the required amount and place in a preheated oven at 180°C for five minutes.

For The Rack Of Mutton

Remove all the fat and season well with salt and pepper. Place in a frying pan on a medium heat. Season the meat and *seal* on all sides, then place in the oven at 170°C for about 15 minutes for medium rare.

> **Chef's Tip**
> Place removed fat on the rack whilst cooking to add flavour.

For The Mash Potato

Drain the peeled and cooked potatoes and mash them whilst adding the cream, butter, salt and pepper.

For The Pea And Mint Purée

Place the chicken stock in a pan and bring to a boil. Add the peas to the chicken stock with the mint. Cook for five minutes and then blend, adding the butter until smooth. Continue cooking on a low heat to reduce and thicken the purée.

For The Summer Vegetables

Prepare and cook the baby vegetables in boiling water and allow them to simmer for five minutes. Remove from the heat and add the butter and salt and pepper to taste.

For The Sauce

Sweat the shallots with rosemary until soft. Add the Madeira and reduce by half, then add the lamb stock and reduce further until the sauce coats the spoon.

To Serve

Assemble as in picture.

RICH CHOCOLATE TART WITH PISTACHIO ICE CREAM

SERVES 12

 Red Muscadel, Nuy
(South Africa)

Ingredients

Pistachio Ice Cream

500ml milk
5ml cream
25g milk powder
25g glucose
125g caster sugar
4 egg yolks
37g butter
5g *trimolene*
70g pistachio paste
(bought by professional pastry chefs from outlets
such as G. Detout)

Tart Case

(makes 2 x 30cm shallow tarts or 1 large tart)

175g butter
350g plain flour
125g caster sugar
2 whole free range eggs

Filling

300g butter
270g dark chocolate
6 eggs
6 egg yolks
450g caster sugar
150g plain flour or ground hazelnuts

Method

For The Pistachio Ice Cream

Cook all ingredients out in a pan until the mixture starts to thicken and it coats the back of a wooden spoon, then remove from the heat.

Pass through a sieve and freeze in a container or ice cream machine.

For The Tart Case

Rub flour and butter and sugar together with your hands until there are no lumps. Add two free range eggs.

Knead pastry with hands until soft and smooth.

Refrigerate for one hour.

Using a floured base and rolling pin roll the pastry to approximately 2cm thick.

Grease tart case with butter.

Line the pastry in the bottom of the case.

Blind bake with greaseproof paper and baking beans for 12 minutes at 180°C until golden brown.

For The Tart Filling

Whisk the eggs, butter and sugar together, and then fold in the flour or ground hazelnuts.

Melt chocolate over a *bain-marie* and mix it in.

Pour the chocolate mixture into the tart case and bake at 180 to 200°C until the top is crisp.

Set in fridge for at least one hour.

> **Chef's Tip**
> Use 80% cocoa chocolate and heat bowl whilst mixing.

To Serve

Serve as in picture.

050
FELLINIS

Church Street, Ambleside, Cumbria, LA22 0BT

015394 32487
www.fellinisambleside.com

Fellinis, an acclaimed modern 'Vegeterranean' restaurant catering for the most discerning palette with a distinctive Mediterranean twist.

When Fellinis opened three years ago local residents were, at first, sceptical about 'another vegetarian restaurant' in Ambleside. We invited them in to sample some gourmet morsels and a chance to have a look round. It didn't take long for our guests to be impressed by the food and ambience. Many friends and regular customers were made that night.

The menu changes regularly to reflect the seasons and availability of local ingredients. Luckily we have the use of an organic kitchen garden at Yewfield, who often supply us with beautiful vegetables and herbs. Our wine list was chosen with great care to complement the flavours of the food, with new additions introduced frequently.

Head chef, Scott Graham, and managing director, Dorothy Smith, spend many hours locked in the kitchen perfecting dishes and menus. They share a passion for new and exciting vegetarian cuisine. Both have been cooking vegetarian food for more than 20 years. Nenad Raicevic (restaurant manager), with his welcoming manner and professional approach, has made Fellinis a very popular venue.

Fellinis also offers a unique studio cinema experience which shows art-house and independent films, and hosts seasons of live performances of theatre, opera and ballet directly via satellite from such prestigious venues as La Scala and The National Theatre.

In total, we have five cinema screens between Fellinis and our award-winning sister restaurant, café and jazz bar 'Zeffirellis', where we also screen the latest blockbusters (including 3D), special interest and foreign language films.

Lovers of food and film can enjoy our great value movie deal, a two course meal and a reserved cinema seat, at any of the cinemas and either restaurant.

Both Fellinis and Zeffirellis, in the delightful market town of Ambleside, offer an evening to remember. Beautifully furnished to reflect the atmosphere of the different venues. Delicious vegetarian food, newly released films, amazing coverage of live ballet, theatre, opera and world class musicians performing regularly. A memorable evening is guaranteed at either of our award-winning establishments.

CARAMELISED GOAT'S CHEESE CANNELLONI WITH CARQUINYOLIS, BALSAMIC & RASPBERRY DRESSING

SERVES 4

 Picpoul de Pinet (Coteaux de Languedoc)
(France)

Ingredients

Goat's Cheese Cannelloni

400g soft goat's cheese
1 bunch chives
2 Braeburn apples
500g caster sugar
500ml water
salt and pepper
a little cream (if necessary)

Carquinyolis

3 eggs
1 cup caster sugar
1 cup plain flour
1 tbsp ground aniseed
1 tbsp ground cinnamon
1¼ tsp active dry yeast
½ lemon (zest)
1¼ cups toasted almonds

Raspberry Dressing

1 tbsp raspberry vinegar (Agnes Rose)
1 tbsp aged balsamic
6 tbsp virgin olive oil
1 tsp Dijon mustard
salt and pepper

Method

For The Goat's Cheese Cannelloni

Combine the water and sugar over a gentle heat to make a light caramel.

Slice the apples very thinly with a mandolin (do not peel) and place them in the caramel. Remove and leave to cool.
Overlap the apple slices on a sheet of baking paper to make a 10" (26cm) by 4" (12cm) rectangle.

Meanwhile, beat the goat's cheese with the chives and season with salt and pepper, add cream to thin if necessary (should be piping bag consistency). Put mixture into a piping bag and pipe down the centre of the apples. Roll up. Leave to set in the fridge for approximately one hour.

Remove from fridge, sprinkle well with caster sugar and glaze with a blow torch.

For The Carquinyolis

Line a baking sheet. Preheat oven to 190°C.

Beat one egg in a small bowl and keep it to one side for now.

Place sugar, flour, aniseed, cinnamon, yeast, and zest in a mixer and beat well with a paddle attachment. Beat in the remaining two eggs, one at a time on high speed, mixing well after each addition. Fold in the almonds.

Turn the dough out onto a well-floured surface and divide it in half. Shape into slightly flattened cylinders about 3" wide by 14" long. Brush off excess flour with a dry pastry brush. Carefully transfer the dough cylinders to prepared baking sheet. Brush the dough cylinders with the beaten egg you have set aside at the beginning of the process.

Bake for approximately 30 minutes, misting the dough with water from a spray bottle every ten minutes or so until the crust is shiny and dark brown. Allow to cool slightly. Slice into half inch thick slices and transfer to a wire rack to allow them to cool completely.

For The Raspberry Dressing

Shake all ingredients together in a screw top jar.

To Serve

Slice the goat's cheese cannelloni and serve with the Carquinyolis and raspberry dressing.

TURKISH STUFFED AUBERGINES ON RED PEPPER, HARISSA SAUCE SERVED WITH COURGETTE & MINT SAUTEED SALAD

SERVES 4

Ribera del Duero (Bodegas Santa Eulalia)
(Spain)

Ingredients

Stuffed Aubergines

2 medium aubergines
100g couscous
stock to cover couscous
5 tbsp olive oil
2 onions (chopped)
4 garlic cloves (chopped)
1 tsp cinnamon (ground)
1 tsp cumin seeds (ground)
50g pine nuts
6 dates (pitted and chopped)
1 tbsp orange flower water
100g peas (defrosted if frozen)
handful of parsley (finely chopped)
1 medium tomato (cut in half)
salt and pepper

Sauce

1 onion (chopped)
2 gloves garlic (chopped)
2 red peppers
1 tsp Harissa paste
1 tbsp tomato purée
2 tbsp olive oil
200ml vegetable stock

Courgette And Mint Salad

2 courgettes (topped/tailed and sliced
lengthways on a mandolin)
handful of mint (finely chopped)
1/2 lemon (juice of)
oil for frying
salt and pepper

Method

For The Stuffed Aubergines

Gently beat the aubergine with a rolling pin. Roll back and forth until slightly collapsed. Make a shallow cut around the stem end without cutting through completely. Twist the top and pull - the core should come out easily. Scoop out any remaining flesh and chop coarsely. Sprinkle the cavity with a little salt and turn upside down to drain.

Put the couscous in a bowl and cover with the stock. Leave to soak for approximately 15 minutes. Meanwhile, heat two tablespoons of oil and fry the cinnamon and cumin slightly, then add the onions, garlic and chopped aubergine. Fry until soft and golden. Transfer to a bowl.

In the same pan, heat a further two tablespoons of oil and fry the pine nuts until golden. Add to the mixture along with the dates, orange flower water, peas, parsley and couscous. Taste and season as appropriate.

Spoon the mixture into the aubergine cavities, pushing in firmly so that they regain their former shape. Push half a tomato in the end to keep the filling in. Brush all over with the remaining oil and place in a roasting tin. Pour in vegetable stock to 1cm depth and drizzle over a little more oil. Cover with tinfoil and roast in a preheated oven 200°C, gas 6 for 30 to 40 minutes until tender.

For The Sauce

Heat the oil and fry the onion, garlic and Harissa paste until the onions are soft. Add the red peppers along with stock and cook until tender. Purée and sieve and keep on one side until ready to serve.

For The Courgette And Mint Salad

Squeeze the lemon juice over the courgettes. Heat the oil in a griddle pan and fry the courgettes until soft and golden, sprinkle over the chopped mint and turn gently. Add a further squeeze of lemon and oil and season to taste.

To Serve

Place a couple of spoons of warm sauce on a plate. Slice the aubergines into rounds and place in sauce. Lightly toss the courgette salad and place at the side.

Bon appétit.

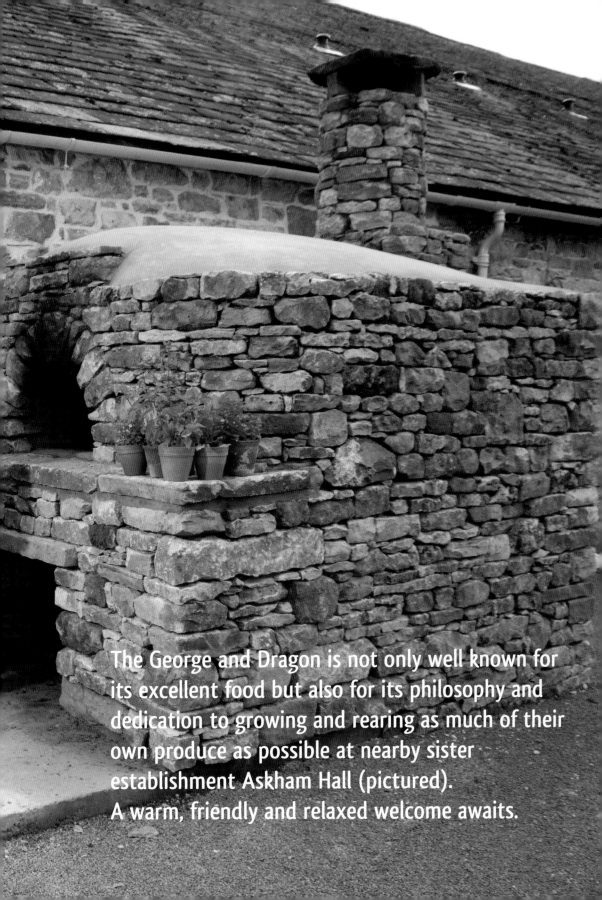

The George and Dragon is not only well known for its excellent food but also for its philosophy and dedication to growing and rearing as much of their own produce as possible at nearby sister establishment Askham Hall (pictured).
A warm, friendly and relaxed welcome awaits.

GRAVADLAX TROUT, ASKHAM BABY BEETS WITH A CIDER & APPLE DRESSING

SERVES 4

 A lovely, flinty Albarino (Spain)

Ingredients

Gravadlax

1kg sea trout (with skin on)
60g sea salt
60g soft brown sugar
20g heather honey
1 lemon (zest)
6 crushed peppercorns
10ml rapeseed oil
1 medium beetroot (grated)

Baby Beets

1kg baby beetroot
20ml rapeseed oil
10ml sherry vinegar
20ml balsamic vinegar (aged 8 years recommended)
pinch of salt

Cider And Apple Dressing

20g Dijon mustard
10g caster sugar
10g cider vinegar
1 Granny Smith apple (diced)
80g mayonnaise
a squeeze of lemon juice

Method

For The Gravadlax
(allow for 12 hours refrigeration time before serving)

Spread a double layer of clingfilm onto your work surface, approximately twice the size of your fish. Sprinkle half of the salt, sugar and lemon zest onto the clingfilm then place the sea trout skin side down on top. Spread the honey and remaining salt, sugar and lemon zest over the fish. Place the peppercorns, rapeseed oil and finally the grated beetroot over the fish, then wrap tightly in the clingfilm. Place the wrapped fish in a tray. The fish must be pressed down whilst being refrigerated using approximately 1kg of weight. I always use a few metal trays from the store cupboard. The fish must be refrigerated for 12 hours, turning over after six. When the fish is ready, remove it from the fridge and wash with cold water. The fish can then be trimmed to neaten the edges before serving.

For The Baby Beetroot

Wash and trim the stalks from the baby beetroots. Place in a pan, cover the beetroots with boiling water and season the water with salt. *Blanch* in the pan for 18 to 20 minutes. Allow the beets to rest for ten minutes before using a small knife to peel them. Marinade in the oil, sherry vinegar and balsamic vinegar for ten minutes until cool.

For The Cider And Apple Dressing

Blitz all ingredients using a handheld blender.

To Serve

Thinly slice the gravadlax and plate up with the baby beetroots and finish by drizzling over the cider and apple dressing.

> **Chef's Tip**
>
> Add homemade croutons for added crunch. Wild, edible flowers and herbs can be used for extra taste and colour.

APPLE & ELDERFLOWER FRITTERS

SERVES 4

 A deep coloured, rich and sweet pudding wine such as Muscat Des Baunes (France)

Ingredients

Fritters

2 Granny Smith apples
(peeled, cored and sliced approx 1cm thick)
6 elderflower heads (pure white)
60g caster sugar
5g cinnamon
$^{1}/_{2}$ltr – 1ltr vegetable oil (depending on size
of pan)

Batter

8 free range egg yolks
8 free range egg whites
500g plain flour
500ml good quality apple cider

Sorbet

600g raspberries (washed)
110g caster sugar

Syrup (Optional)

1ltr water
2kg caster sugar
35 pure white elderflowers
(available to forage June to mid July)
3 lemons (juice and rind)
200ml stem ginger syrup

Method

For The Batter

To make the batter whisk the egg yolks with the apple cider until smooth. Add the flour. Whisk the egg whites to firm peaks then fold into the mix.

For The Sorbet

Pour the caster sugar over the raspberries. Stand for 20 minutes at room temperature then liquidise in a food processor and pass through a fine sieve. Pour into an ice cream machine and churn for 20 minutes.

For The Fritters

Heat the vegetable oil in a fryer or a deep pan to 170°C. Dip the apple slices in batter and cook in the oil for approximately eight to nine minutes until golden brown on both sides. Meanwhile, mix the caster sugar and cinnamon together in a shallow bowl. Lift the fritters out of the oil and place on kitchen paper to drain off any excess oil, then roll the fritters in the caster sugar and cinnamon mix. Repeat the same method for the elderflowers but only cook them for two to three minutes.

To Serve

Arrange the apple fritters on a plate and spoon a portion of sorbet on top, then finish with some elderflower fritters.

Chef's Tip

Pour over some homemade elderflower and ginger syrup for the perfect finish to this pudding.

Method:

Heat water and caster sugar to 50°C. Take off the heat and add 35 pure white elderflowers with the juice and rind from three lemons, then refrigerate for 24 hours. Pass through a muslin cloth then mix 300ml of the syrup with 200ml of stem ginger syrup. Serve hot or cold. Any spare elderflower syrup can be mixed with soda water and used as a refreshing drink or mix with Champagne and garnish with cucumber.

070
GILPIN HOTEL
& LAKE HOUSE

Crook Road, Windermere, LA23 3NE

015394 88818
www.gilpinlodge.co.uk
www.gilpinlife.co.uk

Family owned and run since 1987, Gilpin Hotel & Lake House is a proud member of Relais & Châteaux. Relaxed and unhurried, there are no weddings, conferences or children under seven to disturb the peace, just warm smiles, fresh flowers and friendly, unpretentious service. The interiors are stylish, warm and comfortable, with gorgeous fabrics, art and upholstery.

The three AA Rosette restaurant has four intimate dining rooms where we celebrate some of the finest Lake District produce and West Coast seafood. Traditional British flavours are blended in a light, imaginative way, with delicate flavours and exquisite ingredients that speak for themselves. Carefully matched wines are recommended with each dish and we invite you to wander into the walk-in wine cellars where you can browse over 200 wines from 13 countries, built on interest rather than ancient vintages at astronomical prices.

Gilpin Hotel has 20 gorgeous rooms and suites - half have spa baths and patio doors leading directly onto the gardens, whilst the six garden suites each have a private cedarwood hot tub in their own decked garden.

For the ultimate in luxury, escape to Gilpin Lake House, a Lake District sanctuary where just six suites exclusively share a private swimming pool, sauna, cedarwood hot tub, four acre lake, 100 acres of private grounds, boat-house, kitchen gardens, druids circle, and lake walks leading to panoramic views of the Lake District mountain ranges.

It's time to chill.

WHITE CHOCOLATE CHEESECAKE, POACHED PINEAPPLE, FENNEL ICE CREAM

SERVES 4

 Gaillac Doux Renaissance 2008, Domaine Rottier, Galliac (South West France)

Ingredients

Cheesecake
50g good quality white chocolate
250g mascarpone cheese (room temperature)
100ml whipping cream
32g icing sugar (room temperature)
1¹/₂ leaves gelatine (soaked)

Crumble Base
100g plain flour
75g demerara sugar
85g unsalted butter
15g unsalted butter (melted)

Poached Pineapple
1 small pineapple (cut into wedges)
350g sugar
250ml pineapple juice
1 cinnamon stick
3 star anise
5 cardamom pods (crushed)
2 limes (juice and zest)
1 fresh vanilla pod
500ml water

Caramel Purée
200ml poached pineapple cooking liquid
1 gelatine leaf (soaked)

Fennel Ice Cream
1 fennel bulb (washed and finely chopped)
250ml double cream
1 sprig tarragon
150g sugar
250ml milk
3 egg yolks
250ml semi whipped cream

Fennel Powder
1 large fennel bulb (roughly chopped)
500ml pomace or olive oil
2 star anise
5 sprigs tarragon
250g Ab-Zorbit

Method

For The Cheesecake
Beat the mascarpone and icing sugar by hand until smooth. Heat the cream on medium heat until almost boiling, then whisk in the gelatine. Pour the cream over the chocolate, leave for two minutes to melt together, then mix until smooth. Gradually fold the cream into the mascarpone mix, hand-beating after each addition of cream. Pour into a loose bottomed cake tin lined with greaseproof paper. Refrigerate to set.

> **Chef's Tip**
> Make the cheesecake topping entirely by hand, as it tends to split if using a mixing machine.

For The Crumble Base
Mix the flour, sugar and unmelted butter to a crumbly breadcrumb consistency. Bake at 160°C until golden brown (five to ten minutes). When cool, add the melted butter and spread onto the semi-set cheesecake mix, pressing gently.

For The Pineapple
On a medium heat, caramelise the 250g sugar, cinnamon, star anise, cardamom, lime and vanilla in a pan until a dark golden brown. Mix the pineapple juice, 100g sugar and water together and add to the caramelised sugar and spices. Bring the mix to a boil and add the pineapple. Cook on a low heat until the pineapple is tender. Remove from the heat leaving in the liquid to absorb the flavour.

For The Caramel
Heat the poached pineapple cooking liquid and whisk in the gelatine.

For The Ice Cream
Gently heat the fennel, double cream, tarragon and the 50g sugar in a pan until the fennel is very soft. Blend in a food processor until smooth. Pass through a fine sieve. Heat the milk in a pan to just under boiling point. Whisk the egg yolks and the remaining 100g sugar together then, add the milk and whisk to make a custard. Mix the fennel purée and custard mix together and cool to room temperature. Semi-whip the cream until it just holds a peak. Fold in to the cooled fennel custard, cover and freeze.

For The Fennel Powder
Infuse the fennel, oil, star anise and tarragon on a very low heat for two hours. Pass through a fine sieve and cool the liquid to fridge temperature. Add up to around 250g Ab-Zorbit until it turns into powder. (Ab-Zorbit is a specialist ingredient that can be found online at www.msk-ingredients.com. Adding it to oil turns it to powder - it turns back to liquid once in the mouth.)

To Assemble The Dish
Cut the cheesecake into your preferred shape add diced pineapple and caramel purée around it. Using a hot spoon or ice cream scoop, add the ice cream. Sprinkle over the fennel powder.

080
THE HIGHFIELD HOTEL & RESTAURANT

The Heads, Keswick, Cumbria, CA12 5ER

017687 72508
www.highfieldkeswick.co.uk

Keswick's best kept culinary secret is out!

We opened our hotel restaurant to non-residents so that you could discover the stunning cuisine offered by Head Chef Gus Cleghorn and his talented, international team of chefs.

Our award-winning hotel is in an amazing position overlooking Derwentwater. The grand Victorian villa was built in 1885 using slate quarried in the Borrowdale Valley. It is beautifully proportioned and has many well preserved original features.

We'd love you to join us and admire the magnificent views that can be seen from every window. You'll soon appreciate why we were voted one of the top ten most scenic restaurants in the UK by The Times.

Our chefs choose the best seasonal Cumbrian produce from local suppliers and use their flair and imagination to create a menu that changes every day.

Our head chef, Gus, worked at the Michelin Starred Michael's Nook and the two AA Rosette Wordsworth Hotel in Grasmere before joining us to create perfection night after night. His right hand man is Frenchman Henri Coicadan, a Michelin trained chef, who is a master of desserts.

All the major guidebooks love our food and we're proud to have two AA Rosettes for Culinary Excellence.

Our team design dishes you can enjoy, whatever your dietary requirements - vegetarian, coeliac, gluten free - just let us know when you book.

Why not make a night of it and book one of our 18 en-suite rooms? Each one has been designed and furnished to make the most of its unique features. Our bedrooms offer you the chance to sit in a turret, relax on a veranda or gaze from a balcony! Every room has views of Derwentwater down the Borrowdale Valley, or look towards the mountains.

Our restaurant is the perfect place for a quiet supper or private celebration for up to 40 people.

SMOKED LOCAL SPRINGWATER TROUT PATE WITH SMOKED SALMON, PINK GRAPEFRUIT & POPPY SEED CROUTE

SERVES 4

Head Over Heels Forgotten Riesling
(South East Australia)
A dry Riesling that is a great food match, honeyed
and aromatic but with a citrus finish.

Ingredients

4 x 200g slices smoked salmon (long cut)

Trout Pâté

4 smoked trout fillets (skinless and boneless)
100g full fat cream cheese
20g chopped chives
1 lemon (juice and zest)
1 lime (segments and zest)

Poppy Seed Croûte

2 slices white bread
2 tbsp olive oil
blue poppy seeds

Chardonnay Dressing

4 tbsp olive oil
1 tsp English mustard
1 tsp Chardonnay vinegar
1 tsp hot water

Garnish

1 pink grapefruit (segmented)
1 packet mixed salad leaves

Method

For The Smoked Trout Pâté

In a food processor, combine together smoked trout and cream cheese. Add lemon, lime zest and lime segments and blend until smooth. Stir in the chopped chives and lemon juice to taste.

> **Chef's Tip**
>
> Buy Springwater trout from Riverside Smoked Foods 01946 817 000.

For The Chardonnay Dressing

Put the mustard in the bowl, whisk in one teaspoon of hot water. Add the olive oil slowly, whisking continually, followed by the Chardonnay vinegar.

For The Blue Poppy Seed Croûte

Cut the crusts off the bread and roll each slice (using a rolling pin or a pasta machine) until each one is as thin as possible. Cut into thin strips and place on an oiled baking sheet. Sprinkle with poppy seeds. Place a weighted tray on top of the bread strips (to keep the bread flat). Bake in the oven at 180°C for five to eight minutes or until crisp.

Cooking And Finishing

Divide the smoked trout pâté into four portions. Wrap each portion with a piece of smoked salmon. This should be placed on a bed of mixed leaves in the centre of each plate. The grapefruit segments are placed around the pâté with the dressing. Stick the poppy seed croûtes into the top of the pâté.

ROAST LOIN & HERB CRUSTED CUTLET OF CUMBRIAN SWALEDALE LAMB WITH BUTTER CRUSHED JERSEY ROYAL NEW POTATOES

SERVES 4

Monte Real Reserva 2004, Rioja (Spain)
Benchmark Rioja from one of the finest Bodegas.
A treat for the discerning palate and a perfect
match for lamb.

Ingredients

For The Lamb
4 lamb cutlets (ask your butcher for local lamb
and to clean the cutlet bones for you)
1/2 loin (470 - 500g) local lamb
butter (melted)

Crushed Potatoes
1kg Jersey Royal new potatoes
sea salt and fresh ground black pepper (to taste)
125g butter
1 small bunch spring onions

Herb Crust
4 slices fresh white bread
125g butter
1 bulb fresh garlic (crushed)
20g fresh parsley
20g fresh tarragon
20g fresh sage
1 lemon (zest)
sea salt and fresh ground black pepper (to taste)

Mustard Mix
1tbsp French mustard
5g fresh rosemary (chopped)
1 bulb fresh garlic

Minted Thyme Jus
100ml lamb stock
100ml port
10g fresh mint
10g fresh thyme
the juices from the cooked lamb

Garnish
8 baby carrots
8 mangetout
8 fine beans

Method

Preheat the oven to 200°C, 400°F or gas 6.

For The Herb Crust

Put the herbs, lemon zest and fresh bread in a blender and blitz
until the breadcrumbs are bright green.

Place the butter and one bulb of crushed garlic into a pan
and soften without colouring. Add the breadcrumb mix and fry
briefly. Remove from heat to cool.

For The Mustard Mix

Mix together the mustard, one bulb of crushed garlic and
chopped rosemary in a bowl.

For The Crushed Potatoes

Wash the potatoes, leaving the skins on. Place in a pan of water,
bring to a boil and cook for 15 to 20 minutes. Drain well.
Return the potatoes to the pan, add the butter and cover.

Whilst the lamb is cooking, reheat the potatoes, crush and
season with sea salt and pepper. Add the spring onions.

> **Chef's Tip**
> Add fresh parmesan to the potatoes to make them sticky.

For The Lamb Loin

Brush the loin and the cutlets with melted butter. Season with
sea salt and black pepper. In a hot frying pan, fry the loin fat
side down for 30 seconds, turn and fry the other side until
browned. Do the same with the cutlets, 30 seconds each side or
until brown.

Place the loin on a roasting tray, fat side down, brush with the
mustard mix and roast for five minutes. Prior to serving, the lamb
should be removed from the oven and left to 'rest' for five minutes.

For The Lamb Cutlets

Place the cutlets on a baking tray and brush with the mustard
mix, press the herb crust into this mix and roast for five
minutes. Remove from the oven and 'rest' for five minutes
before serving.

For The Minted Thyme Jus
Using the meat juices from cooking, add the port and reduce
by half. Add the lamb stock, reduce again by half. Finally, add
the mint and thyme to the *jus*, pass through a sieve and serve.

To Serve
Assemble as in the picture.

KESWICK BAKED SULTANA CHEESECAKE WITH WALNUT MAPLE SYRUP

SERVES 8

Vistamar Late Harvest Moscatel (Chile)
Made from Moscatel grapes that have been
allowed to become very ripe. Sweet and rich but
with a clean marmalade character.

Ingredients

Cheesecake Base

125g digestive biscuits
125g ginger nut biscuits
50g butter

Cheesecake Topping

225g caster sugar
3 tbsp cornflour
675g full fat soft cheese
2 eggs
1 tsp vanilla essence (or seeds from one vanilla pod)
300ml whipping cream
75g chopped sultanas (soaked overnight in a little brandy, rum or whisky)

Sauce

397g tin condensed milk
splash of maple syrup
125g chopped walnuts (or alternatively pecan nuts etc)

Method

Preheat oven to 180°C, 350°F or gas 4.

Butter a 10" loose bottom cake tin and line sides with greaseproof or silicone paper. DO NOT line the base.

For The Base

Use a food processor to blend the biscuits together into a fine crumb. Melt the butter and mix with the biscuit crumbs.
Press into the bottom of the cake tin to approximately a quarter of an inch in thickness.

For The Topping

Mix the sugar and the cornflour together, beat in the full fat soft cheese until creamy in texture. Beat in the eggs and vanilla essence and fold through the chopped sultanas. Slowly pour in the whipping cream and beat for ten minutes to ensure a light fluffy topping.

Pour the mixture into the cake tin and place the tin in the oven in a water bath (approximately an eighth of an inch of water surrounding the tin). Bake in the oven for 40 to 50 minutes until golden brown. Check the cheesecake is cooked by placing a knife through the centre - if the knife is clean when removed then it is cooked.

For The Sauce

Place the unopened tin of condensed milk in a pan and cover it completely with water. Gently boil in the pan for a minimum of two hours. Let it cool completely. The condensed milk should be brown in colour and of a toffee consistency when the tin is opened.

Gently heat the maple syrup in a microwave and add the chopped walnuts.

Add one tablespoon of condensed milk per serving to the maple syrup and serve with the cheesecake.

Chef's Tip

Try using peanuts or hazelnuts for a different taste. Alternatively, for a nut free alternative, add one spoon per serving of whipped cream to the condensed milk (toffee sauce) to make a toffee cream.

For a gluten free alternative, use gluten free biscuits to form the cheesecake base.

090
HOLBECK GHYLL

Holbeck Lane, Windermere, Cumbria LA23 1LU

015394 32375
www.holbeckghyll.com

Some people visit the Lake District for the heart-stopping scenery, others come for the acclaimed food. Standing proudly over Windermere, the charming Holbeck Ghyll combines the two in a way that no other hotel can.

Recognised as one of the best restaurants in the North and with a reputation for food and service that extends far overseas, it is little wonder this charming 19th Century Arts and Crafts house has been granted a Michelin Star for 12 consecutive years.

The man responsible for this rare achievement is head chef David McLaughlin, who took the helm of the oak-panelled restaurant just five months after it was awarded its first star. While he's on the radar of food critics far and wide, for those less in the know David is something of an unsung hero, preferring to shy away from the limelight to concentrate on serving excellent food - locally sourced where possible - in the most mouth-wateringly imaginative way.

One of the most extensive wine cellars in the region, put together by Holbeck's award-winning sommelier, and views that gaze over Lake Windermere and the fells, make this the ultimate destination for serious food fans.

Time your visit right and you may find yourself dining next to a national food writer, or taking afternoon tea in one of the plush lounges while a Hollywood A-Lister warms her toes by the fire.

Fuss-free but put together with the fiercest attention to detail, the food has been worthy of a Michelin Star for 12 consecutive years, but it's not just the restaurant that's internationally acclaimed. While its own mantelpiece is full of silverware (including gongs for an adventurous 300-strong wine list), the hotel was recently awarded Small Hotel Of The Year in the Cumbria Tourism Awards. Situated high on a hill, overlooking Lake Windermere and the Langdale Pikes, Holbeck Ghyll boasts a view so intoxicating Andrew Harper voted it

BUCKWHEAT BLINIS WITH SMOKED SALMON & HORSERADISH CREME FRAICHE

SERVES 6 PEOPLE WITH PLENTY OF CANAPES

Pinot Gris Tradition, Hugel, 2007, Alsace (France)

Method

For The Blinis

Mix together the flour, baking powder and salt.

Mix the egg yolks with the milk then pour into the flour mix. Whisk the egg whites until they form soft peaks and fold them into the batter. To cook, heat a non-stick pan and brush with oil. Drop teaspoon sized amounts of the batter into the pan. Cook until golden brown then turn and do the other side. Leave to cool.

Chef's Tip

If pushed for time the blinis can be made the day before and kept in an airtight container in the fridge.

For The Horseradish Crème Fraiche

Mix the horseradish relish and crème fraiche together.

To Serve

Twist the slices of smoked salmon into rounds and place on each blini. Put a small amount of the crème fraiche in the middle. Garnish with fresh dill sprigs, lime segments - or caviar if you are feeling extravagant!

Ingredients

Blinis

6 large slices of smoked salmon
200g buckwheat flour (sieved)
1/2 tsp baking powder
1/2 tsp salt
2 egg whites
2 egg yolks
200ml milk

Horseradish Crème Fraiche

125g crème fraiche
1 tsp horseradish relish

Garnish

dill
lime segments
caviar (optional)

FILLET OF ABERDEEN ANGUS BEEF WITH PUY LENTILS & HORSERADISH GNOCCHI

SERVES 4

 Cabernet Sauvignon - Art Series, Leeuwin Estate, 2006, Margaret River (Western Australia)

Ingredients

4 x 170g fillet steaks (and trimmings)

Puy Lentils

2 carrots (finely diced)
¹/2 celeriac (finely diced)
¹/2 swede (finely diced)
100g puy lentils
sherry vinegar
8 slices pancetta
large knob of butter

Gnocchi

6 shallots (finely chopped)
280g plain flour
¹/2 pint vegetable stock
250g butter
7 eggs
2 dtsp horseradish relish
(or 1 inch finely grated fresh)
salt and pepper

Port Sauce

¹/2 bottle port
¹/2 bottle red wine
3 shallots (sliced)
2 cloves garlic
4 pints chicken stock

To Serve

1 bag baby spinach (wilted)
225g mixed wild mushrooms
olive oil

Roasted Vegetables

olive oil
Chantenay carrots
baby red onions
butternut squash

Method

For The Gnocchi

Melt the butter in a pan, add the shallots and cook until soft. Add the vegetable stock and bring to a boil then add the flour and beat over the heat for a few minutes. Slowly add the eggs, one at a time, then season with a little salt and pepper and add the horseradish.

Transfer mixture into a piping bag and squeeze out portions into simmering water, cutting off sections with the back of a knife. Simmer for a few minutes and allow to cool.

For The Puy Lentils

Place the lentils in cold water and bring to a boil. Drain off and cover again with cold water, add root vegetables and sliced pancetta and simmer until soft. To finish, put a couple of spoons of the lentils into a pan with a knob of butter, heat through and *deglaze* by adding a few drops of sherry vinegar.

For The Port Sauce

Caramelise the beef fillet trimmings and add three sliced shallots and two cloves of garlic. Cook until brown. Add half a bottle of port and half a bottle of red wine. Reduce right down to a very syrupy consistency, then add four pints of chicken stock and reduce down to a sauce consistency.

For The Roasted Vegetables

Peel and shape the vegetables. *Blanch* in hot water for eight minutes. Panfry in olive oil to give some colour for approximately three minutes. Roast in the oven at 200°C for 45 minutes.

For The Mushrooms

Panfry in olive oil for three minutes and add to the vegetables in the oven when there are 15 minutes remaining.

To Cook The Steaks

Panfry until golden brown all over and finish in a preheated oven at 200°C for five minutes for a rare steak, eight to ten minutes for medium and 12 minutes for well done.

> **Chef's Tip**
> If trimming a whole piece of beef fillet, wrap it tightly in many layers of clingfilm to give it a better shape.

To Serve

Spoon the lentils on the plate and place the wilted spinach on top. Slice the beef and arrange on the plate. Place the roasted vegetables and wild mushrooms around the beef and drizzle with the port sauce.

Hidden in the idyllic valley of Borrowdale, The Leathes Head offers so much more than a warm welcome, award-winning food and stylish interiors- it is a place where guests can relax, nurture their soul and invest in their wellbeing.

LUCYCOOKS COOKERY SCHOOL

Mill Yard, Staveley, Nr Kendal, Cumbria, LA8 9LR

01539 822507
www.lucycooks.co.uk

LucyCooks Cookery School is located in one of the most picturesque areas of Great Britain - the heart of the English Lake District. Its position in the centre of Staveley's Mill Yard couldn't be more convenient, with excellent parking, surrounded by the Kentmere Fells, overlooking the River Kent and nestled amongst a group of artisan businesses. Sandwiched between the brewery and the bakery, LucyCooks is a destination for budding cooks and food lovers alike, as an 'alternative cookery activity' and for those wishing to 'dine with a difference'.

Our 'demo and dine' evenings are now a firm favourite with both locals and visitors alike. Rather like a culinary book club, without the homework! There is plenty of opportunity to take a look at the stunning kitchens upstairs, which accommodates up to 24 people and where all the 'practical' courses are undertaken (including a purpose built station for those who 'can't stand to cook'). LucyCooks' afternoon teas, as well as 'Cupcake And Macaroon Afternoons' are hugely popular as more and more people recognise the value of enjoying a proper English tea with cakes, scones and other such temptations. There's plenty of opportunity to ask questions and enjoy the recipes and handy hints provided to try at home.

As you would expect, LucyCooks offers a wide range of fully practical courses, as well as Demo And Dines, dining with a difference together with bespoke events, team based challenges and family fun days.

Our website has all the details, but please feel free to call in or speak to us about 'booking and cooking with LucyCooks'!

Shortlisted for Europe's Best Cookery School and featured in many magazines and TV programmes, LucyCooks is proud to work with some dedicated food lovers and experts, from chefs to producers, champions of local food and globe trotting delights. There's a course for all reasons and all seasons at LucyCooks.

MACKEREL THREE WAYS SERVED WITH BEETROOT SALAD & HORSERADISH CREME FRAICHE

SERVES 4

 Chateau Bauduc Sauvignon Blanc (France)

Ingredients

Mackerel Rillettes

3 fillets smoked mackerel
(bones and skin removed)
2 fillets fresh mackerel
60g unsalted butter (room temperature)
1 clove garlic
50ml natural yoghurt
1 tsp horseradish cream
pinch paprika
lime juice
salt and pepper

Soused Mackerel

4 fresh mackerel fillets

Pickling Liquid

1 red onion (thinly sliced)
1 tbsp allspice berries
200ml white wine vinegar
250g caster sugar
3 bay leaves
375ml water

Grilled Mackerel

4 fresh mackerel fillets
olive oil
salt
lemon juice

Garnish

beetroot salad
horseradish infused crème fraiche
sour dough bread (toasted)

Method

For The Mackerel Rillettes

Season the fillets of fresh mackerel with salt and place it in a foil envelope with 10g of the butter and a couple of slices of garlic. Cook in the oven at 200°C for eight minutes or until just cooked. Remove from the oven and set aside to cool. When cool, remove the garlic, skin and bones. Reserve the cooking juices for later.

Place the remaining butter in a bowl along with the smoked and cooked fish. Using a fork, mix the fish into the butter until evenly mixed and a fine texture. Add the remaining ingredients and the cooking juices to the bowl and fold together. Adjust the seasoning with the lime juice salt and pepper.

For The Soused Mackerel

To make the pickling liquid, put all of the pickling ingredients into a pan and bring to a boil with 375ml of water. Remove from the heat and allow to cool. Now place the mackerel fillets into a dish they just fit in, and pour over the pickling liquid. Cover the dish and allow to cure overnight.

For The Grilled Mackerel

Preheat a heavy based non-stick frying pan over a medium heat. Add enough olive oil to coat the base of the pan. Season the fish with salt and place skin side down in the pan and cook for two to three minutes. Turn over and cook flesh side down for two minutes. Remove from the pan and season with lemon juice.

Serving Suggestion

Serve together with toasted sour dough bread, a horseradish infused crème fraiche and diced beetroot salad.

> **Chef's Tip**
> Trout works just as well for this dish and is equally delicious.

CUMBRIAN PORK PLATE WITH CRUSHED MINTED PEAS & CELERIAC PUREE

SERVES 4

 Denbies Estate, Flint Valley, Surrey (England)

Ingredients

Belly Pork
1kg square cut belly pork
1 ltr chicken stock
salt and pepper (to season)

Cumberland Eggs
4 quails eggs
150g Cumberland sausage meat
2 eggs (beaten)
plain flour
breadcrumbs

Pork Fillet
4 medallions of pork
(one fillet split into 4 equal portions)
plain flour
mustard powder

Celeriac Purée
1 medium sized celeriac
knob of butter
salt and pepper (to season)

Crushed Mint Peas
150g frozen peas
3 sprigs mint
1 tbsp rapeseed oil

Chef's Tip
Try using British rapeseed oil instead of olive oil - it's lighter, healthier and has a higher smoking point when cooking and it has far less of a carbon footprint being local!

Method

For The Belly Pork
First remove the skin from the pork belly, to use to make crackling spears.

For the belly pork, season and place in a roasting tray. Pour over the boiling stock and wrap in foil. Cook in the oven at 110°C for approximately three hours.

Remove from the oven and drain off the stock. Keep this for sauce. Put a layer of clingfilm on the pork when cool enough and place another tray on top. Place in the fridge overnight with a weight piled on top.

To serve, remove the pork from the fridge and take out of the tray. Trim off the edges neatly and cut into four even squares. In a large frying pan, heat some olive oil until hot and then fry the pork, fat side down until golden brown. Turnover and finish heating in a hot oven, 200°C.

For The Pork Scratchings
Cut the pork skin into even sized strips. Salt them heavily and then place on a baking tray, place another tray on top of this to stop them curling up. Put into a hot oven to crisp at 220°C for 30 to 45 minutes.

For The Cumberland Eggs – Bon Bon Style
Simmer the quails eggs for two minutes. Remove from the pan and place into cold water to stop the cooking. Peel the eggs, cover in sausage meat and then *pane* in the flour and breadcrumbs. Deep fry at 180°C until golden brown.

For The Pan Seared Pork Fillet
Pat the pork medallions with the flour and then season with salt and the mustard powder.

In a very hot, large, deep, heavy frying pan, *seal* the pork fillet with lots of colour, place into a hot oven, 200°C and roast for eight minutes. Allow to rest for five minutes before serving.

For The Celeriac Purée
Peel and chop into cubes a medium sized celeriac, then cook in water until tender. Season and put into a blender with a knob of butter (1cm square) until smooth.

For The Crushed Mint Peas
Cook the peas as per instructions adding three sprigs of mint leaves and stems to the water. Then, using a fork, roughly crush the peas with a tablespoon of rapeseed oil.

To Serve
Place the pork belly onto the celeriac purée and assemble as per the picture .

Michael Hudson leads the culinary team at Lucy's, where they are all encouraged to translate local ingredients into eclectic dishes using ideas from the past to influence dishes in the present day and the future. Lucy's believes that, whilst the food is important, good food goes hand in hand with all the other things you need to experience when dining out - whether you dine alone or in company - Lucy's On A Plate creates a memory worth savouring from start to finish.

HAM HOCK & WILD MUSHROOM TERRINE WITH A SCOTCH EGG & PEASE PUDDING

SERVES 4

 Chilean Sauvignon Blanc – a nice blend of fruit and acidity – ideal with this dish

Ingredients

Ham Hock Terrine

2 ham hocks
150g wild mushrooms
banana shallot (finely diced)
50g unsalted butter
large gherkin (finely diced)
salt and pepper (to taste)
1 tsp cumbrian grain mustard
vegetable stock
(enough to cover the ham hocks completely)

Scotch Egg

1 banana shallot (finely chopped)
250g lean pork mince
4 quail eggs (cooked and peeled)
sage leaves (finely chopped)
salt and pepper (to taste)
300g fine breadcrumbs
1 egg (beaten)
100g plain flour

Pease Pudding

500g yellow split peas
(soaked overnight in cold water)
1 onion (peeled and quartered)
1 carrot (peeled and quartered)
2 tbsp white wine vinegar
sea salt and white pepper
20g unsalted butter (cut into cubes)

Method

For The Ham Hock Terrine

Boil hocks in a pan with the stock for one to two hours until the meat is tender and falling off the bone. Remove from the stock and allow to cool. Once cooled, remove fat and bones, shred the ham.

Melt butter and sweat the shallots and mushrooms. Allow to cool before mixing with the shredded ham in a bowl. Add the gherkin and mustard and continue to combine the mixture. Season to taste.

Press the mixture into four small terrine dishes. Cover with clingfilm and refrigerate for two to three hours (or overnight) before serving.

Chef's Tip

Reserve some of the cooking stock from the hocks to cook the split peas in for extra flavour, but be careful not to over season if you do this.

For The Scotch Egg

Place mince in a mixing bowl and mix with the sage, shallot and seasoning. Mould a small amount around each quail's egg to a thickness of approximately 4mm.

Roll in the flour, then the beaten egg and finally the breadcrumbs.

Deep fry for four to six minutes on 170°C or bake in the oven for 20 minutes at 180°C.

For The Pease Pudding

Drain the soaked peas and tip into a saucepan. Add the onion and carrot and cover with water. Bring to a boil and simmer gently for an hour or until the peas are tender. Cool slightly and then skim anything from the surface.

Discard the onion and carrot and blitz to a purée in a blender. Pour into a clean pan. Add the vinegar and season to taste.

Beat in the butter gradually a cube at a time.

Chill before serving.

To Serve

Assemble as per the photograph (filo pastry sail and green pea purée optional!).

LOIN OF VENISON WITH MINIATURE CUMBERLAND PIE & TURNIP FONDANT

SERVES 4

*Chateau Bauduc Cabernet Merlot.
From the estate belonging to Lucy's brother ,
Gavin Quinney between Bordeaux and St Emilion
(France)*

Ingredients

Cumberland Pie

400g venison mince
2 carrots (peeled and diced)
2 sticks celery (diced)
100g chestnut mushrooms
2 shallots
50g petit pois
4 sprigs fresh thyme
salt and freshly milled pepper
125ml red wine
1 tbsp tomato paste
rich venison or beef stock (to bind)
2 tbsp olive oil (for frying)
100g Cumberland farmhouse cheese
(grated, for gratinating)

Mashed Potato

3 large potatoes
3 tbsp olive oil
salt and pepper

Venison Fillets

4 x 125g venison fillets
sea salt and cracked black pepper

Turnip Fondant

1 - 2 turnips (depending on size)
30g butter
vegetable stock

Method

For The Olive Oil Mashed Potato

Boil and mash the potatoes with the olive oil and season to taste. The olive oil is very much healthier and more flavoursome in this dish than butter and cream.

For The Cumberland Pie

Heat oil in a heavy based pan. Brown the venison mince with shallots, mushrooms, thyme and diced carrot and celery. Add red wine and reduce.

Add tomato paste and simmer for ten minutes. Add a good meat stock (preferably venison). Stir in the petit pois and season to taste.

Place into four metal rings or miniature casserole dishes and top with olive oil mashed potato.

Sprinkle with Cumberland farmhouse cheese and bake for 20 minutes at 180°C.

Venison Fillets

Season the meat using sea salt and cracked black pepper. *Seal* in a hot pan until all coloured. Cook for ten minutes in a preheated oven at 180°C. Rest for 15 minutes under silver foil before serving.

Turnip Fondant

Peel and cut the turnip into a round circle approximately one and a half centimetres high and place in a tray half immersed with vegetable stock.

Butter the top of the turnip and place in the oven at 160°C. Bake for one and a half hours until the top is golden brown and the turnip softly cooked.

To Serve

Present the venison on top of the turnip fondant and alongside the Cumberland pie.

Used turned vegetables to accompany for example beetroot, swede and carrot.

Chef's Tip

You could also make this using fillet of beef and best minced beef for the pie. Be careful not to overseason.

SAUCY LEMON PUDDING WITH LIMONCELLO MERINGUE ICE CREAM

SERVES 6

 Brown Brothers Late Picked Orange Muscat (Australia), or more Limoncello!

Ingredients

Saucy Lemon Pudding

60g unsalted butter (softened)
250g caster sugar
4 eggs (separated)
2 tsp finely grated lemon zest
50g self raising flour
350ml milk
80ml lemon juice
icing sugar (to serve)

Limoncello Meringue Ice Cream

4 egg whites
225g caster sugar
300ml double cream
2 lemons (grated rind)
1 lemon (zest)
2 tbsp limoncello liqueur
1 tbsp lemon curd

Method

For The Saucy Lemon Pudding

Heat the oven to 180°C (gas mark 4). Grease six ramekin dishes.

With an electric mixer, beat the butter, half of the sugar, the egg yolks and the lemon zest until the mixture is light and fluffy. Alternately fold in the flour and mix through the milk to make a smooth batter. Stir in the lemon juice. The batter may look like it has separated at this stage, but this is as it should be.

In a separate, clean bowl, whisk the egg whites until frothy. Continue to whisk while adding the remaining sugar, a little at a time, until it's all incorporated and is firm and glossy. Gently fold the egg white mixture into the batter.

Pour the batter into the prepared dish. Place the dish in a large baking tin and fill the tin with enough lukewarm water to come a third of the way up the side of the dish. Gently transfer it to the oven and bake for 50 to 55 minutes, or until the top is golden and risen. Dust with icing sugar and serve.

For The Limoncello Meringue Ice Cream

Whisk the egg whites until stiff. Add the caster sugar a spoonful at a time until meringue is really stiff. Spoon into even sized dollops and place on silicone paper and cook for three hours on a low heat (110°C).

Whip the cream until of a soft dropping consistency. Add the limoncello and fold in the lemon curd. Stir in the zest and rind of the lemons.

Crush the cooled meringues into pieces (not powder) and stir into the cream mixture (don't worry, as you fold it together it binds together well). Transfer the mixture into a polythene tub and freeze.

To Serve

Assemble as shown with the limoncello meringue ice cream, a mango purée 'stripe' and a shot of limoncello liqueur with a cinammon stick for show!

> **Chef's Tip**
>
> The limoncello prevents the ice cream from freezing rock hard so it can be served straight from the freezer!

A regular in the Good Food Guide, the two AA rosette Punch Bowl has been the recipient of numerous past awards including the prestigious Michelin Pub Of The Year in the 2009 Michelin Guide, a Cesar Award for Cumbrian Inn Of The Year in the Good Hotel Guide 2010 and was named one of the Top 10 Gastro Pubs in the country.

Head chef Scott Fairweather was recently named Cumbria's Young Chef Of The Year 2012 and he has brought renewed energy, vision and excitement to the Punch Bowl's menus with a real focus on ingredients that can be found or foraged locally.

SEARED LOCH FYNE SCALLOPS, ROASTED CAULIFLOWER, PARMA HAM, CAPER & GOLDEN RAISIN PUREE

SERVES 4

La Crema Chardonnay, Sonoma Coast, 2007
(California)

Ingredients

Purée
100g lilliput capers
300g golden raisins
water

Poached Apples
1 Granny Smith apple
25ml white wine
25g granulated sugar
25ml water

Scallops
12 Loch Fyne medium king scallops
$^1/_2$ lemon (juice)
curry salt
2 tbsp rapeseed oil
50g unsalted butter

Garnish
4 slices air dried ham
12 pea shoots
12 small cauliflower florets
2 tbsp rapeseed oil

Method

For The Purée
Cover the capers and golden raisins in water in a medium saucepan and bring to a boil for two to three minutes until the fruit is plump. Pour into a food processor and blend until smooth. Pass through a fine sieve and store in a squeezy bottle.

For The Poached Apples
Using a melon baller, scoop out 12 spheres from the un-peeled apple. Bring the water, white wine and sugar to a boil, add the apples to the pan and simmer until tender and slightly translucent.

For The Garnish
Blanch the cauliflower florets in salted water until *al dente*, drain and then roast in a hot oven with two tablespoons of rapeseed oil until golden.

Lay out the air dried ham between baking trays lined with greaseproof paper. Bake at 180°C for 15 to 20 minutes until crisp and allow to cool.

For The Scallops
Season the scallops with curry salt and sear over a medium heat in a non-stick pan until golden on one side. Turn each one, add a knob of unsalted butter to the pan and the juice of half a lemon and then remove from the heat. Allow to rest for one minute in the pan before serving, basting with the foaming butter during this time.

To Serve
Assemble as in picture. Garnish with pea shoots.

> **Chef's Tip**
> Adjust the presentation to suit your taste. Cauliflower purée, streaky bacon and crispy sage would also work well.

CUMBRIAN LOIN OF LAMB, SHEPHERD'S PIE, BROAD BEANS, PEAS, MINT JELLY

SERVES 4

🍷 *Hares Breath Pinot Noir, Muddy Water, South Island, 2008 (New Zealand)*

Ingredients

Lamb And Shepherd's Pie
200g minced lamb or mutton
1 banana shallot
1 carrot
1 stick celery
1 leek (white only)
1 clove garlic
1 bay leaf
1 sprig rosemary (leaves removed and chopped)
1 small glass red wine
1 ltr lamb stock
4 x 2" x 2" savoury pastry cases
(can be bought from good supermarkets)
200g creamed potato
1 Cumbrian fell bred loin of lamb

Carrot Purée
800g carrot (peeled and finely diced)
400ml double cream
50g unsalted butter
1 tbsp rapeseed oil
salt and ground white pepper

Mint Jelly
225g water
150g white wine vinegar
50g caster sugar
1 tbsp mint sauce
2 gelatine leaves

Lamb *Jus*
20ml rapeseed oil
1 white onion, 1 carrot (peeled and diced)
2 sticks of celery (diced)
1 leek (white part only, diced)
1 bulb of garlic
2 star anise, 6 black peppercorns, 6 fennel seeds
1 bay leaf, 1 sprig rosemary, 1 sprig thyme
1kg lamb bones
1 large glass of Merlot
2 ltrs of good quality beef/lamb stock
1 lemon

Garnish
fresh peas and broad beans

Method

For The Carrot Purée
Sweat down the carrot in one tablespoon of rapeseed oil until softened. Add the cream and butter and simmer until the carrot begins to break down and the liquid has reduced. Blend to a smooth purée, pass through a fine sieve and season with salt and ground white pepper to taste.

For The Mint Jelly
Line a square 500ml jelly mould with a double layer of clingfilm and leave to one side. Place all ingredients into a saucepan and bring up to 80°C, stirring continuously to dissolve the gelatine. Pour into the prepared mould and leave to set for 20 minutes before cutting into a 2cm dice.

For The Shepherd's Pie
Fry the lamb mince in small batches over a high heat to render down the fat, remove to one side. Finely dice all of the vegetables and sweat down over a medium heat until softened. Add the mince back to the pan and *deglaze* with red wine. Cover with the lamb stock and simmer for one hour until the meat is tender and the sauce has reduced.

Assemble the meat on the four savoury pastry cases, pipe on creamed potato and bake in the oven at 180°C for 12 to 15 minutes until golden.

For The Lamb Loin
Remove the layer of fat from the loin and trim away any excess sinew. Divide into four portions, around 200 to 220g each. Sear in a hot pan on all sides. Roast in the oven at 180°C for six to eight minutes (for medium-rare).

> **Chef's Tip**
> Rest the lamb loin for half of the overall cooking time before carving. The same would apply for any meat when roasting.

For The Lamb *Jus*
Roast the lamb bones in the oven for one hour at 180°C until browned. Sweat the vegetables in the oil over a high heat until browned, stirring continuously to prevent them from burning. Add the aromatics to the pan, followed by the roasted lamb bones, then the red wine and reduce until the liquid has almost evaporated. Add the beef or lamb stock and simmer gently for two to three hours until it has reduced to the right consistency which should just coat the back of a spoon. Skim any fat from the surface of the sauce frequently for best results. When ready, pass the *jus* through a fine sieve to remove all of the vegetables and bones and then pass again through a muslin cloth to remove any impurities. Finish the sauce with seasoning and lemon juice.

To Serve
Serve with fresh peas and broad beans, mint jelly and lamb *jus*.

BITTER CHOCOLATE TART, LYTH VALLEY DAMSON PUREE, PISTACHIO TUILE

SERVES 12 - 16 (1 whole tart)

🍷 *Pedro Ximenez Sherry, Lustau (Spain)*

Ingredients

Pastry

300g plain flour
150g unsalted butter
1 pinch of salt
2 tbsp icing sugar
2 tbsp ground almonds
2 eggs

Chocolate Ganache

620g double cream
2 bay leaves
550g 70% dark chocolate callets

Pistachio Tuile

300g caster sugar
60g green pistachios

Garnish

Lyth Valley damson purée
green pistachios (chopped)
Maldon sea salt
vanilla ice cream

Method

For The Pastry

Place the flour, salt, butter, almonds and icing sugar in a food processor and pulse to a fine breadcrumb. Add the eggs and blend briefly until the mix binds together. Turn out onto a floured surface, knead to a ball and rest for 30 minutes in the fridge. Roll out onto a greased, 12 inch tart case and *blind bake* at 180°C until golden, removing the baking beans after around eight minutes.

For The Ganache

Heat the cream and bay in a saucepan and leave to infuse for 20 minutes. Pass through a fine sieve onto the chocolate callets and stir until melted and smooth. Pour into the baked pastry case and set in the fridge (preferably overnight).

For The Pistachio Tuile

Place the sugar and pistachios in a saucepan and gently heat to a golden caramel. Carefully pour out onto silicone mats and leave to set. Transfer the brittle caramel to a food processor and blend to a fine nougatine powder. Using a round cutter, sprinkle the powder into thin discs, again on a silicone mat and place in the oven at 180°C for three to five minutes until the sugar has melted once more. Allow to cool before serving or store in an airtight container for up to two days.

To Serve

Serve a slice of the chocolate tart with vanilla ice cream, one tuile, damson purée and chopped green pistachios.

> **Chef's Tip**
> Slice the tart using a hot, sharp knife and serve immediately for the best result.

150
THE SAMLING HOTEL

Ambleside Road, Windermere, Cumbria, LA23 1LR

01539 431 922
www.thesamlinghotel.co.uk

The Samling Hotel offers guests some of the finest modern British cuisine that you will find anywhere in the North. The chefs at The Samling are consistently producing contemporary food to achieve stunning presentation and a balanced taste. The Samling has 11 superbly appointed bedrooms, giving their guests the opportunity to stay over and enjoy the extensive wine list or the famous seven course gourmand tasting menu with wine pairing that complements the food beautifully. The ever popular hotel restaurant has stunning elevated views of Lake Windermere. When combined with discreet service so effortless it is hardly noticed, it's easy to see why The Samling Hotel is rapidly becoming one of the most popular intimate hotspots of the North once again.

The Samling has won numerous Michelin Stars
and AA Rosettes over the years, continuing its
philosophy of using the finest and freshest locally
sourced ingredients cooked to perfection.
The hotel's four course lunch menu is gaining
admirers by the day and is regularly described as
one of the best value, award-winning meals in
the whole of the North of England.

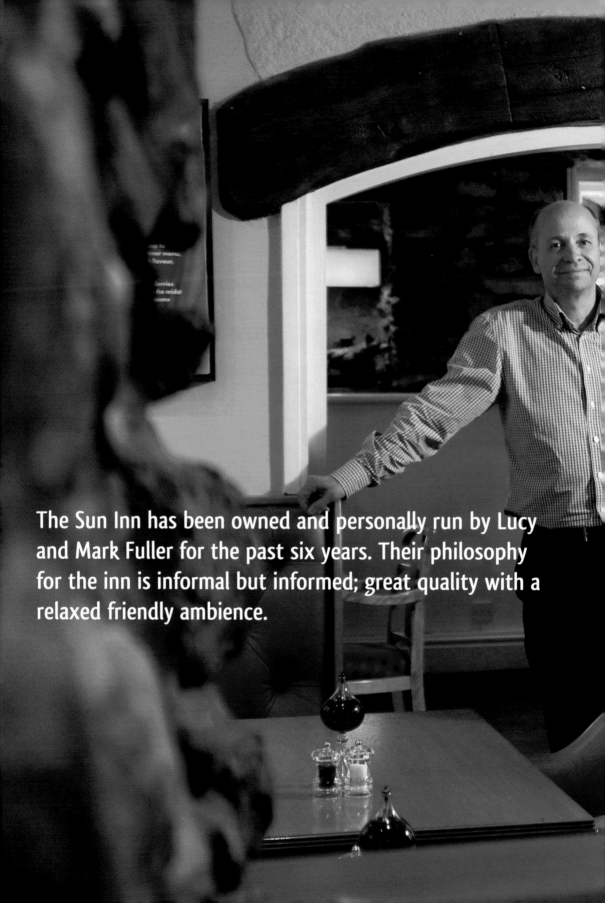

The Sun Inn has been owned and personally run by Lucy and Mark Fuller for the past six years. Their philosophy for the inn is informal but informed; great quality with a relaxed friendly ambience.

HAM HOCK & CHICKEN TERRINE

SERVES APPROXIMATELY 12 STARTER SIZE SLICES

*Moment de Plaisir, Vin de Pays d'Oc, Languedoc
(France)*

Ingredients

For The Ham Hocks

2 large or 3 small ham hocks
2 onions
1 bulb garlic
4 carrots
4 sticks celery
1 leek
1 tbsp black peppercorns
2 bay leaves
a few sprigs of fresh thyme and rosemary

To Build The Terrine

2 chicken breasts
2 large carrots (cut into long batons)
1 small head spring cabbage (sliced thinly)
2 gelatine leaves (softened in cold water)
1 tbsp wholegrain mustard
1 onion (finely diced and sautéed in vegetable oil)
small bunch of parsley (finely chopped)
pinch of white pepper

Method

For The Ham Hocks And Chicken

To cook the ham hocks, roughly chop all the vegetables and put into a large pan with the ham hocks. Add the garlic, peppercorns, bay leaves, thyme and rosemary. Cover with water, bring to a boil, turn down the heat and cook slowly for a few hours, until tender.

Meanwhile, roast the chicken breasts, leave to cool and then cut into strips, like goujons. *Blanch* the carrot batons and cabbage and set aside.

When the ham hocks are ready, remove from the stock. Reserve 500ml of the stock and discard the rest along with the vegetables. Stir the gelatine leaves into the hot ham stock and set aside. When the meat is cool enough to handle, pick the meat from the bones and place in a bowl along with the sautéed onion, mustard, parsley and pepper and combine. Check the seasoning, but you probably won't need any as the ham hocks are quite salty.

To Assemble The Dish

Line the terrine mould with clingfilm, leaving some hanging over the edges so you have enough to wrap up the terrine. Start with a layer of the ham mixture and then alternate it with layers of the prepared chicken and vegetables, finishing with a layer of the ham mixture. Pour the reserved ham stock over the filling and cover with the overlapping clingfilm. Put in the fridge with an even weight on the top (this helps the terrine set firmly) and leave overnight. When ready to serve, slice and serve with homemade piccalilli and freshly toasted bread.

Chef's Tip

Use the remaining ham stock to make a tasty pea and ham soup for a warming supper.

170
TROUT HOTEL

Crown Street, Cockermouth, Cumbria, CA13 0EJ

01900 823 591
www.trouthotel.co.uk

The four star Trout Hotel, where more than £3m has been invested in recent years, boasts an award-winning restaurant, a bistro and bar and 49 luxurious well-appointed bedrooms.

Based in Cockermouth, the Trout was recently placed in the top four large hotels in the country at the Visit England Awards For Excellence 2012.

It offers five completely different dining experiences, each offering extensive menus to suit all tastes. All have one thing in common - delicious, fresh food.

The choice comprises the award-winning Derwent Restaurant, ideal for a romantic dinner, the Lounge Bar for a light bite and The Terrace Bistro, a more contemporary setting perfect for lunch with the option of dining alfresco on The Terrace. The hotel can also provide private dining in the luxurious surroundings of the Wordsworth Room.

Everything is cooked fresh on the premises by head chef Alex Hartley and his dedicated team, all of whom are extremely passionate about the countryside.

The hotel is committed to supporting the local economy and is proud of the provenance and quality of its food with the emphasis being on home grown and locally sourced ingredients.

As a result, the chefs source produce from the surrounding area, ranging from cheese made from Cumbrian milk to free range pork from local farms.

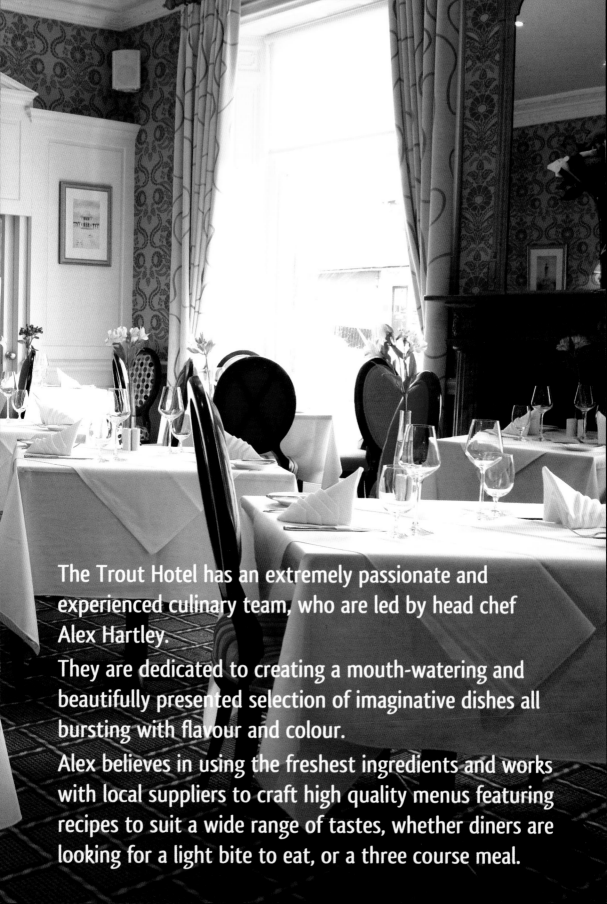

The Trout Hotel has an extremely passionate and experienced culinary team, who are led by head chef Alex Hartley.

They are dedicated to creating a mouth-watering and beautifully presented selection of imaginative dishes all bursting with flavour and colour.

Alex believes in using the freshest ingredients and works with local suppliers to craft high quality menus featuring recipes to suit a wide range of tastes, whether diners are looking for a light bite to eat, or a three course meal.

LAKELAND PANCETTA & MUSHROOM TART, TOPPED WITH SCALES FARM EGG, DRIZZLED WITH SUNBLUSHED TOMATO DRESSING

SERVES 6

 Chardonnay/Viognier 'The Ruins' Bon Cap Estate (South Africa)

Ingredients

Pastry
375g plain flour
60g salted butter
60g lard
pinch salt
140ml water

Filling
200g Lakeland pancetta
200g mushrooms (sliced)
2 sprigs parsley (chopped)
3 eggs
140ml double cream
140ml milk
pinch salt and pepper

6 eggs (to poach)

Dressing
30ml vegetable oil
10ml white wine vinegar
100g sunblushed tomatoes
1 tsp Dijon mustard
pinch salt, pepper and sugar
36 baby spinach leaves

Method

For The Pastry
Rub together the sieved flour, lard, butter and salt. Slowly add the 140ml water until the mix forms a ball. Leave to rest in the fridge. Roll out the pastry and cut into six using five inch tart cases, then *blind bake* for 12 minutes on 170°C.

> **Chef's Tip**
> *Blind bake* the tart cases using coins as they conduct the heat better.

For The Filling
Slice and fry the pancetta, then cook with the sliced mushrooms and add to tart cases. In a jug, whisk up the eggs, cream, milk, salt, pepper and parsley and fill each tart case covering the mushrooms and pancetta.

Bake in the oven for 12 minutes at 160°C.

For The Dressing
While the tarts are cooking, whisk together the vinegar, Dijon mustard, salt, pepper and sugar, then slowly add the oil whilst whisking. Then add the chopped sunblushed tomatoes.

To Serve
Arrange baby spinach leaves on plate, place a warm tart on top of the spinach leaves, top with soft poached egg and drizzle with sunblushed tomato dressing.

LINE-CAUGHT WILD SEABASS WITH KING PRAWN, SPINACH & TARRAGON ORZOTTO

SERVES 4

 Dart Valley Reserve 2011, Sharpham Estate, Totnes, Devon (England)

Ingredients

4 x 200g line-caught wild seabass fillets
olive oil
knob of butter
pinch salt and pepper

Orzotto

250g pearl barley
10 raw king prawns
50g butter
50g parmesan
280ml vegetable stock
1/2 onion
100g spinach
sprig tarragon (chopped)

Garnish

100g rocket
100ml olive oil
50g fresh basil

Method

For The Garnish

Warm the olive oil, add the fresh basil leaves and blitz. Reserve until needed.

For The Orzotto

Melt the butter and add the finely chopped onion, then add the pearl barley, ensuring that the barley is coated with the melted butter. Add a little of the stock whilst stirring and, when pearl barley has absorbed the stock, add more stock a little at a time until the pearl barley is cooked. Then add the chopped raw king prawns, grated parmesan, washed spinach and tarragon. Season to taste.

For The Fish

Heat a non-stick pan with a little olive oil and place the seabass skin side down in the pan to cook for three minutes. Then add a knob of butter, turn over and baste the fish with the butter in the pan. Cook for a further two to three minutes.

> **Chef's Tip**
> Score the skin side of the fish to make it cook faster and more evenly.

To Serve

Place orzotto mix on the plate, seabass fillets to the side and sit the rocket on top of the orzotto and drizzle with the basil oil.

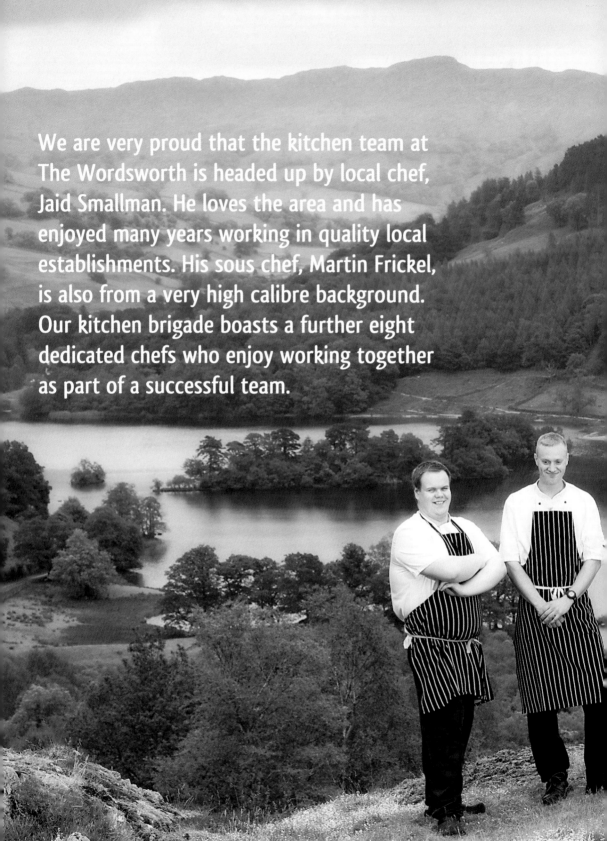

We are very proud that the kitchen team at The Wordsworth is headed up by local chef, Jaid Smallman. He loves the area and has enjoyed many years working in quality local establishments. His sous chef, Martin Frickel, is also from a very high calibre background. Our kitchen brigade boasts a further eight dedicated chefs who enjoy working together as part of a successful team.

CRISP COD CHEEKS, SALT COD PANNA COTTA, CARROT MOUSSE, SMOKED PANCETTA POWDER, RED VEIN SORREL

SERVES 4

Oppenheimer Herrenburg Reisling, Kabinett,
Rhinehessen, 2007 (Germany)
Wine Recommendation: Will Hurst, Restaurant Manager

Ingredients

Crisp Cod Cheeks

8 cod cheeks
200g Panko breadcrumbs
4 eggs
150ml milk
200g flour

Salt Cod Panna Cotta

200g salt cod
125ml milk
250ml double cream
lemon juice
2^1/$_2$ leaves gelatine

Carrot Mousse

8 carrots (peeled and chopped)
50g butter
170ml double cream
1 leaf bronze gelatine (soak in white wine)

Pancetta Powder

100g pancetta
2 tbsp smoked olive oil
100g tapioca *maltodextrin*

Pickled Carrot

4 carrots
300ml white wine vinegar
300g caster sugar

Garnish

red vein sorrel
chive flowers

Method

For The Carrot Mousse

Peel and finely chop the carrots, place in a medium saucepan with butter and a pinch of salt and submerge with water. Simmer slowly with a lid on for 15 minutes, reduce liquid by half. When the carrots are soft, blend in a food processor until glossy and smooth, chill in refrigerator to be used later.

Measure 400g of carrot purée, soak the gelatine and dissolve in the white wine, then add to the purée. Whip the cream to stiff peaks and fold into the purée. Season the mousse with salt and pepper, reserve in fridge for later.

For The Salt Cod Panna Cotta

Place the cod, cream and milk in a small saucepan. Bring the liquid to a boil - this will cook the fish. Add the soaked gelatine, then place into a liquidiser, blend until smooth. Pass through a fine sieve and season with lemon. Pour into 2cm round silicone moulds and reserve in fridge until later.

For The Pickled Carrot Ribbons

Cut the edges of the carrots to produce a square shaped carrot, thinly slice on a mandolin to produce thin ribbons. Bring the sugar and vinegar to a boil and pour over the ribbons, cover and allow to cool.

For The Cod Cheeks

Place the cod cheeks into the seasoned flour, then into beaten egg, then into the breadcrumbs. Reserve until ready to serve.

For The Pancetta Powder

Finely chop the pancetta, fry gently in the smoked olive oil to release the oil from the pancetta. Once nice and crisp, drain the pancetta and allow the oil to cool.

Once cool, slowly whisk the oil into the tapioca *maltodextrin* to create a loose powder. Finely chop the crisp pancetta add to the powder, season and reserve.

To Serve

Gently fry the cod cheeks and assemble as pictured.

ANNA'S HAPPY TROTTERS ORGANIC PORK, SEA KALE SHOOTS, FONDANT POTATO, FORAGED WOODLAND MUSHROOMS, COWMIRE HALL CIDER JUS

SERVES 4

Chenin Blanc, Jordan, Stellenbosch, 2011
(South Africa)
Wine Recommendation: Will Hurst, Restaurant Manager

Ingredients

Pork

1 Anna's pork shoulder
500g Anna's pork loin
2 onions
1/2 head celery
4 carrots
300ml white wine

Fondant Potatoes

4 Maris Piper potatoes
200g butter
300ml chicken stock
thyme and garlic

Sauce

400ml Cowmire cider
1 ltr veal and pigs trotter *jus*

Garnish

100g foraged mushrooms
(chanterelles are recommended)
cabbage flowers
200g sea kale shoots
12 baby carrots
100ml carrot purée

Method

For The Pork Shoulder

Pot roast the shoulder on the bone with the wine and vegetables for five to six hours at 160°C (part cover the pot). Gently remove the skin, fat and bones and *vac pack* tightly. Press in the vac bag until chilled and set. Slice into rectangles and panfry for serving.

For The Pork Loin

Fully trim the pork loin and place in a vacuum bag. Cook *sous vide* at 62°C for 20 to 30 minutes. Remove from the bag and *seal* in a pan until a good caramelisation is achieved, carve and serve.

For The Fondant Potatoes

Cut the potatoes into cylinders. Panfry in butter to achieve colour on the surface. Turn them over and add garlic and thyme. Pour over the chicken stock and cook out gently for 18 to 20 minutes.

For The Sauce

Reduce the Cowmire Hall cider by four fifths until it is an intensely flavoured syrup. Add this to taste to the veal *jus* base.

To Serve

Panfry the woodland mushrooms, *blanch* the sea kale leaves and shoots and the baby carrots and assemble all of the elements on four plates as in the picture.

ANNE FORSHAW'S YOGHURT MOUSSE, SWEET CLOVER MERINGUE, ENGLISH RASPBERRY TEXTURES

SERVES 4

🍷 *Late Harvest Semillon Gewürztraminer,*
Casa Silva, 2007 (Chile)
Wine Recommendation: Will Hurst, Restaurant Manager

Ingredients

Mousse

600g strained yoghurt
30g Melilot plants (sweet clover)
1^1/$_2$ ltrs double cream
7 leaves gelatine
150g caster sugar
1 lemon (zest and juice)

Meringue

250g egg whites
500g caster sugar
125ml water
30g freeze dried raspberries
20g dried Melilot

Raspberry Vinegar Jelly

200ml raspberry vinegar
400ml stock syrup (400g caster sugar, 400ml water, bring to boil, chill)
7g agar agar

Garnish

1 punnet fresh raspberries
fresh Melilot flowers

Method

For The Yoghurt Mousse

Add the zest and juice of a lemon to the yoghurt, then take a small saucepan, add the sugar and Melilot. Submerge with water and bring to a boil, add the gelatine and dissolve. Allow to cool before adding to the yoghurt. Whip the cream to form stiff peaks and fold into the yoghurt mixture, then reserve.

For The Melilot Meringue

Place the sugar and water in a saucepan and bring to 115°C. Softly whip the egg whites, then gradually pour the syrup into the egg whites to create a stiff meringue, keep whisking until cold.

Spread thinly onto baking parchment, sprinkle with freeze dried raspberries and dried Melilot.

Place into a dehydrator or low oven for eight to ten hours.

For The Raspberry Vinegar Jelly

Combine the raspberry vinegar, stock syrup and agar agar in a small saucepan. Bring to a boil, whisking frequently.

Pour onto an oiled baking sheet around 4cm deep. Allow to cool and refrigerate. The jelly can be diced into 1.5 x 1.5cm squares once set.

To Serve

Place half the fresh raspberries in the freezer until completely frozen, then smash with a rolling pin. Assemble as pictured.

BAKERY & CONFECTIONERY

BELLS BAKERS LIMITED
www.bellsoflazonby.co.uk
Edenholme Bakery, Lazonby, Penrith, Cumbria, CA10 1BG.

Bakery products including breads and cake slices.

BRYSONS OF KESWICK
www.brysonsofkeswick.co.uk
42 Main Street, Keswick, Cumbria, CA12 5JD.

Wide range of breads, cakes, morning goods and cream cakes. Specialities include Lakeland plum bread and Borrowdale tea bread.

CARTMEL STICKY TOFFEE PUDDING CO LTD
www.cartmelvillageshop.co.uk
The Square, Cartmel, Cumbria, LA11 6QB.

Sticky toffee pudding, sticky ginger pudding and sticky banana pudding.

CLASSIC DESSERTS LTD
www.classicdesserts.co.uk
Units 19-21 Blencathra Business Centre, Threlkeld Quarry, Keswick, Cumbria, CA12 4TR.

Handmade desserts and puddings including sticky toffee pudding, cheesecake, tortes, pies and cakes.

COUNTRY FARE
www.country-fare.co.uk
Country Fare, Mallerstang, Kirkby Stephen, Cumbria, CA17 4JT.

Handmade biscuits, cakes, speciality puddings and pickles.

COWMIRE HALL
www.cowmire.co.uk
Crosthwaite, Cumbria, LA8 8JJ.

Supplier of fantastic cider and damson gin.

GRASMERE GINGERBREAD
www.grasmeregingerbread.co.uk
Church Cottage, Grasmere, Ambleside, Cumbria, LA22 9SW.

Gingerbread and traditional Cumberland rum butter.

LITTLE SALKELD WATERMILL
www.organicmill.co.uk
The Watermill, Little Salkeld, Penrith, Cumbria, CA10 1NN.

Organic and bio-dynamic flours.

LUNESDALE BAKERY
50 Main Street, Kirkby Lonsdale, Cumbria LA6 2AJ.

Produce artisan bread, pastries, cakes and pies.

MOODY BAKER CO-OP
www.themoodybaker.co.uk
3 West View, Front Street, Alston, Cumbria, CA9 3SF

Breads, cakes, snacks and biscuits.

MORE? THE ARTISAN BAKERY
www.moreartisan.co.uk
More? The Artisan Bakery, Mill Yard, Staveley, Nr Kendal, LA8 9LR.

A continuously evolving range of artisan breads and seasonal desserts.

BEVERAGES

AQUA PURA
www.aqua-pura.com
Cumbrian natural mineral water.

BEDROCK GIN
www.bedrockgin.co.uk
Bedrock Gin, Spirit of the Lakes Ltd, Keswick, CA12 5SQ.
Gin crafted from the natural spring water of the Lake District and botanicals.

CORNEY AND BARROW WINES
www.corneyandbarrow.com
Sedbury Stables, Sedbury Hall, Richmond
North Yorkshire, DL10 5LQ.
At 230 years old, Corney & Barrow is one of the longest established Independent Wine Merchants in the UK.

DENT BREWERY LTD
www.dentbrewery.co.uk
Hollins, Cowgill, Dent, Cumbria, LA10 5TQ.
A fine selection of Cumbrian beers, as served in the George and Dragon.

ENNERDALE BREWERY
www.ennerdalebrewery.co.uk
Croasdale Farm, Ennerdale, Cumbria, CA23 3AT.
Beer made with traditional methods, for modern tastes.

HARDKNOTT BREWERY
www.hardnott.com
Unit 10, Devonshire Road Trading Estate, Millom, LA18 4JS.
A selection of Cumbrian beers.

HAWKSHEAD BREWERY
www.hawksheadbrewery.co.uk
Hawkshead Brewery Ltd, Mill Yard, Staveley,
Cumbria, LA8 9LR.
A selection of Cumbrian beers.

HIGH CUP WINES
www.highcupwines.co.uk
Townhead Farm, Keisley, Murton, Appleby-in-Westmorland,
Cumbria, CA16 6NF.
Country wines made from fruit.

JENNINGS
www.jenningsbrewery.co.uk
Jennings Brewery, Castle Brewery, Cockermouth,
Cumbria, CA13 9NE.
A selection of Cumbrian beers.

J FARRER & CO LTD
www.farrers.net
13 Stricklandgate, Kendal, Cumbria, LA9 4LY.
One of the oldest blenders and roasters of the finest teas and coffee.

KENDAL CORDIALS
www.kendalcordials.co.uk
A selection of cordials and fruit drinks.

KESWICK BREWING COMPANY
www.keswickbrewery.co.uk
The Old Brewery, Brewery Lane, Keswick, CA12 5BY.
Craft beer that is available in anything from bottles to 18 gallon casks.

MITCHELL KRAUSE BREWING
www.mkbrewing.co.uk
PO Box 86, Workington, Cumbria, CA14 9BD.
Beer made in a variety of continental and American styles.

STRINGERS BEER
www.stringersbeer.co.uk
Unit 3, Low Mill Business Park, Ulverston, LA12 9EE.
These beers are produced in a small, family run brewery with 100% renewable energy.

WILLOW WATER
www.willowwater.com
Natural mineral water.

DAIRY, CHEESE, MILK & ICE CREAM

APPLEBY CREAMERY
www.applebycreamery.com
Appleby Creamery Ltd, Units 3A/B, Cross Croft,
Appleby-in-Westmorland, Cumbria, CA16 6HH.

Wide selection of award-winning cheeses.

CHURCHMOUSE CHEESES
4 Market Street, Carnforth, Kirkby Lonsdale,
Carnforth, LA6 2AU.
www.churchmousecheeses.com

*A superb selection of local, British and continental gourmet
cheeses available to buy online, with a vast range of
Cumbrian fare.*

ENGLISH LAKES ICE CREAM
www.lakesicecream.com
The Old Dairy, Gilthwaiterigg Lane, Kendal,
Cumbria, LA9 6NT.

Luxury dairy ice cream and real fruit sorbets.

HARTLEYS ICE CREAM
www.hartleys-icecream.co.uk
24 Church Street, Egremont, Cumbria, CA22 2AW.

50 flavours of homemade ice cream.

MAWSONS OF BAILEYGROUND
www.mawsonsofbaileyground.co.uk
Seascale, Cumbria, CA20 1NG.

Locally produced milk, butter, smoothies and cheese.

THE CHEESE LARDER
www.cheeselarder.co.uk
Unit 3, Crook Road, Kendal, Cumbria, LA8 8QJ

*Specialist wholesalers of cheese and sundries to the areas
most prestigious hotels and restaurants.*

THE LAKE DISTRICT CHEESE COMPANY
www.lakedistrictcheesecompany.co.uk
Selection of Cheddar cheeses.

THORNBY MOOR DAIRY
www.thornbymoordairy.co.uk
Thornby Moor Dairy, Crofton Hall, Thursby, Carlisle,
Cumbria, CA5 6QB.

*A range of cows, goats and ewes milk cheeses using raw
milk sourced from single herds within Cumbria.*

WARDHALL DAIRY
www.wardhalldairy.co.uk
Ewe Close Farm Arkleby, Wigton, Cumbria, CA7 2DS.

Range of cheese, butter and curds and whey.

WASDALE CHEESE
www.campingbarns.co.uk

Produces various ewes milk cheeses.

WINDERMERE ICE CREAM COMPANY LIMITED
www.scoopchocice.co.uk
12 The Banks, Staveley, Kendal, Cumbria, LA8 9NE.

Ice cream and sorbets.

FRESH PRODUCE

CUMBRIA FRESH PRODUCE LTD
2b George Moor Industrial Estate, Fletchertown, Wigton,
Cumbria, CA7 1BA
www.cumbriafreshproduce.com
Fruit and vegetable wholesalers

EVA'S ORGANICS
www.evabotanicals.co.uk
Medburn, Milton, Brampton, Cumbria, CA8 1HS.
Suppliers of organic fruit and vegetables.

FORAGER
www.forager.org.uk
*Supplier of many interesting ingredients including wild
mushrooms and melilot.*

FOUR SEASONS FOODS
www.4seasonsfoods.com
Threlkeld Business Park, Threlkeld, Keswick,
Cumbria, CA12 4SU.
Fresh local fruit and vegetables.

LOW SIZERGH BARN
www.lowsizerghbarn.co.uk
Low Sizergh Farm, Sizergh, Kendal, Cumbria, LA8 8AE.
*Fruit and vegetables, local where possible. In addition,
the farm shop is filled with a selection of local and
speciality foods.*

LOW STANGER FARM
www.lowstanger.co.uk
Stanger, Cockermouth, Cumbria, CA13 9TS.
Wide range of vegetables and apples from the orchard.

PARSONS OF KENDAL
www.parsonsofkendal.co.uk
Station Yard, Station Road, Kendal, Cumbria, LA9 6BT.
Fruit and vegetables, local where possible.

THE LAKES FREE RANGE EGG COMPANY
www.lakesfreerange.co.uk
The Lakes Free Range Egg Co Ltd, Meg Bank, Stainton,
Penrith, Cumbria, CA11 0EE.
Free range eggs.

MEAT, POULTRY, GAME & FISH

ANNA'S HAPPY TROTTERS
www.annashappytrotters.com
Burland, Holme Road, Howden, East Yorkshire, DN14 7LY.
Supplier of organically produced pork.

BORROWDALE HERDWICK LAMB
www.borrowdaleherdwick.co.uk
Yew Tree Farm, Rosthwaite, Borrowdale, Cumbria, CA12 5XB.
Meat worthy of it's origins in the heart of the Lakes.

CRANSTONS LIMITED
www.cranstons.net
Ullswater Road, Penrith, Cumbria, CA11 7EH.
*High quality local produce including ready meals, sausages,
pies, bacon and fresh meats.*

DALES TRADITIONAL BUTCHERS
www.dalesbutchers.co.uk
2 Market Street, Kirkby Lonsdale, Cumbria LA6 2AU.
*As well as providing excellent local meat, Dales Butchers
has an award-winning range of pies and sausages, all
available online.*

DALES BUTCHERS
www.dalesbutchers.co.uk
2 Market Street, Kirkby Lonsdale, LA6 2AU.

Sausages, black pudding and an array of meat cuts.

DEER AND DEXTER
www.deer-n-dexter.co.uk

Selection of Dexter beef and venison meat products.

DELICIOUSLY WILD
www.deliciouslywild.co.uk
Red Lion House, Gamblesby, Penrith, Cumbria, CA10 1HR.

Free range and additive free venison.

FURNESS FISH, POULTRY AND GAME SUPPLIES
www.morecambebayshrimps.com
Moor Lane, Flookburgh, Grange-over-Sands,
Cumbria, LA11 7LS.

Morecambe Bay potted shrimps, game, smoked meats, poultry, fish, pastries and desserts.

HIGGINSONS LIMITED
www.higginsonsofgrange.co.uk
Higginsons Butchers, Keswick House, Main Street, Grange
over Sands, Cumbria, LA11 6AB.

Pies, sausages, bacon and hams plus local salt marsh lamb from Morecambe Bay and free range and organic poultry and rare breed pork.

LAKES SPECIALITY FOODS
www.lakesspecialityfoods.co.uk
5 Bankside Barn, Crook Road, Staveley, Cumbria, LA8 9NH.

Fully traceable, high quality meats.

MANSERGH HALL FARM
www.manserghhall.co.uk
Kirkby Lonsdale, via Carnforth, Lancashire, LA6 2EN.

Organic lamb and beef, rare breed Saddleback pork, handmade sausage, dry-cured bacon and gammon.

PLUMGARTHS FARMSHOP
www.plumgarths.co.uk
Lakelands Food Park, Kendal, Cumbria, LA8 8QJ.

Local beef, lamb, pork and poultry, as well as chutneys and free range eggs.

RICHARD WOODALL LIMITED
www.richardwoodall.com
Cranswick plc, 74 Helsinki Road, Sutton Fields,
Hull, HU7 0YW

Traditional Waberthwaite Cumberland sausage, dry-cured Cumberland Hams, air dried Cumberland hams, pancetta and bacons etc.

SAVIN HILL FARM
www.savin-hill.co.uk
The Barn, Savin Hill, Lyth Valley, Kendal, LA8 8DJ.

Rare breed British White Beef and Middle White Pork, Saddleback Pork.

SILLFIELD FARM
www.sillfield.co.uk
Endmoor, Kendal, Cumbria, LA8 0HZ.

Dry cured bacon, Cumberland and wild boar sausages, Cumberland dry cured hams, hand raised pies, prosciutto, salamis, black pudding and a range of naturally smoked products.

YEW TREE FARM
www.heritagemeats.co.uk
Coniston, Cumbria, LA21 8DP.

Old fashioned meat. Such as Herdwick lamb, hogget, mutton and belted Galloway beef.

PIONEER FOODSERVICE
www.pioneerfoodservice.co.uk
Fresh meats and other groceries.

PRESERVES, CONDIMENTS & HONEY

CLAIRE'S HANDMADE
www.claireshandmade.co.uk
Miller Park, Station Road, Wigton, Cumbria, CA7 9BA.
Chutneys, jams, marmalades, pickles and piccalilli.

CUMBERLAND MUSTARD
www.cumberlandmustard.com
16 Hill House Lane, Alston, Cumbria, CA9 3TN.
Honey mustards and a range of pickles and vinaigrettes.

FRIENDLY FOOD AND DRINK
www.friendlyfoodanddrink.co.uk
Unit 1, Staveley Mill Yard, Staveley, Nr Kendal,
Cumbria, LA8 9LR.
Diabetic friendly range of preserves, chutneys and coulis.

HAWKSHEAD RELISH COMPANY
www.hawksheadrelish.com
The Square, Hawkshead, Cumbria, LA22 0NZ.
Handmade relishes and pickles.

NOOK FARM HONEY
www.nookfarmhoney.co.uk
Nook Farm, Bailey, Newcastleton, Cumbria, TD9 0TR.
A selection of Cumbrian speciality honeys.

WILD AND FRUITFUL
www.wildandfruitful.co.uk
Hillside, Cuddy Lonning, Wigton, Cumbria, CA7 0AA.
Handmade jams, jellies, chutneys, oils, vinegars and salts.

SMOKED MEAT

LUNE VALLEY SMOKE HOUSE
www.lunevalleysmokehouse.co.uk
Kirby Lonsdale Road, Arkholme, Carnforth, LA6 1BQ.
Quality meats, olives and truffles.

James Goodall, Dale Lodge Hotel & Tweedies Bar

Leon Whitehead, Merewood Country House Hotel & Restaurant

BORROWDALE GATES HOTEL
Grange In Borrowdale, Keswick, CA12 5UQ
017687 77204
www.borrowdale-gates.com

THE CASTLE DAIRY RESTAURANT
26 Wildman Street, Kendal, Cumbria, LA9 6EN
01539 733 946
www.castledairy.co.uk

CRAGWOOD COUNTRY HOUSE HOTEL & RESTAURANT
Windermere, Cumbria, LA23 1LQ
015394 88177
www.cragwoodhotel.co.uk

DALE LODGE HOTEL & TWEEDIES BAR
Red Bank Road, Grasmere, Cumbria, LA22 9SW
015394 35300
www.dalelodgehotel.co.uk

FELLINIS
Church Street, Ambleside, Cumbria, LA22 0BT
015394 32487
www.fellinisambleside.com

GEORGE AND DRAGON
Clifton, Near Penrith, Cumbria, CA10 2ER
01768 865 381
www.georgeanddragonclifton.co.uk

GILPIN HOTEL & LAKE HOUSE
Crook Road, Windermere, LA23 3NE
015394 88818
www.gilpinlodge.co.uk www.gilpinlife.co.uk

THE HIGHFIELD HOTEL & RESTAURANT
The Heads, Keswick, Cumbria, CA12 5ER
017687 72508
www.highfieldkeswick.co.uk

HOLBECK GHYLL
Holbeck Lane, Windermere, Cumbria LA23 1LU
015394 32375
www.holbeckghyll.com

LEATHES HEAD HOTEL
Borrowdale, Keswick, Cumbria, CA12 5UY
01768 777247
www.leatheshead.co.uk

Scott Fairweather, The Punch Bowl Inn & Restaurant

Jaid Smallman, The Wordsworth Hotel Signature Restaurant

LUCYCOOKS COOKERY SCHOOL
Mill Yard, Staveley, Nr Kendal, Cumbria, LA8 9LR
01539 822507
www.lucycooks.co.uk

LUCY'S ON A PLATE
Church Street, Ambleside, Cumbria, LA22 0BU
015394 32288
www.lucysofambleside.co.uk

MEREWOOD COUNTRY HOUSE HOTEL & RESTAURANT
Windermere, Cumbria, LA23 1LH
015394 46484
www.merewoodhotel.co.uk

THE PUNCH BOWL INN & RESTAURANT
Crosthwaite, The Lyth Valley, Cumbria, LA8 8HR
015395 68237
www.the-punchbowl.co.uk

THE SAMLING HOTEL
Ambleside Road, Windermere, Cumbria, LA23 1LR
01539 431 922
www.thesamlinghotel.co.uk

THE SUN INN
6 Market Street, Kirkby Lonsdale, LA6 2AU
01524 271 965
www.sun-inn.info

TROUT HOTEL
Crown Street, Cockermouth, Cumbria, CA13 0EJ
01900 823 591
www.trouthotel.co.uk

THE WORDSWORTH HOTEL SIGNATURE RESTAURANT
Stock Lane, Grasmere, Cumbria, LA22 9SW
015394 35592
www.thewordsworthhotel.co.uk

RELISH PUBLICATIONS

Relish Publications is an independent publisher of exclusive regional recipe books, featuring only the best and brightest critically acclaimed chefs and the venues at which they work, all of which showcased with superb photography. They also work with some chefs individually to produce bespoke publications tailored to their individual specifications. Since 2009, Relish has fostered a national presence, while maintaining friendly, personalised service that their small but highly professional team prides themselves on.

Visit www.relishpublications.co.uk and check out the series of high quality recipe books.

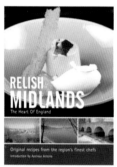

Relish Midlands

As the geographical heart of the country and one of its most densely populated areas, the Midlands has so much to offer in terms of amazing food that blends a variety of styles and influences. The Michelin starred Andreas Antona introduces us to 26 of the best restaurants in the UK.

Relish Wales

A region with its own rich, unique heritage and home to a vast and diverse landscape. From the rugged valleys and endless coastlines to the bustling streets of Cardiff and it's other big cities, Welsh cuisine represents a blend of cultures that is as interesting as it is delicious. Renowned chef Shaun Hill introduces this ambitious book that covers the wide range of talent that Wales has to offer.

Relish Greater Manchester and Cheshire

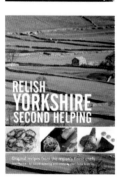

As one of the most populated areas in the UK, Greater Manchester has a wealth of talent to display. Traditionally seen as a historic centre of industry, Manchester's finer side inspires great chefs such as Andrew Nutter to produce truly amazing food. Alongside this, Cheshire offers a refreshing change of pace. Further away from the hustle and bustle, its own character is reflected in some equally stunning cuisine. This Relish book shows it all in this journey around the North West.

Relish Merseyside and Lancashire

As one of the most historically significant ports in the country, Liverpool continues to have importance to this day, by giving us all access to a world of high quality food, but there is just as much talent further afield, as shown in the stunning chefs we have chosen to represent Lancashire. Renowned local chef, Paul Askew, starts off this book by introducing us to some of the quality produce that this region has to offer, and how he is so proud to be championing an area that has many great chefs and restaurants.

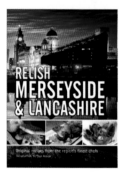

Relish Yorkshire Second Helping

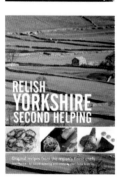

The latest edition of Relish Yorkshire features a foreword by celebrity chef Tessa Bramley and returns to the county with all new recipes from Yorkshire's greatest chefs; Michelin starred James McKenzie from The Pipe and Glass and Steve Smith from The Burlington, plus Richard Allen from The Fourth Floor at Harvey Nichols and many, many more. Relish Yorkshire Second Helping is a must have for any hearty food lover with true Yorkshire pride.

Relish Scotland

With over 300 pages of Scotland's finest recipes, this book takes you on an epic journey from Edinburgh to Glasgow, across to Aberdeen and then up to the Highlands and Islands, through rugged landscapes and beautiful cities. An introduction from TV celebrity chef Nick Nairn prepares the palate for recipes from nationally acclaimed restaurateurs such as Tom Kitchin, Martin Wishart and Geoffrey Smeddle. With breathtaking pictures of the views and venues, Relish Scotland promises to make for fascinating reading for both foodies and tourists alike.

Relish Cumbria Vol. 1

Over 50 mouth-watering exclusive recipes for you to try at home from some of Cumbria's finest Country House Hotels and acclaimed restaurants including Nigel Mendham at The Samling, Russell Plowman at Gilpin Lodge Hotel and Andrew McGeorge at Rampsbeck Country House Hotel. Packed with innovative recipes and stunning photography to match the stunning landscape, Relish Cumbria is certain to make a fantastic addition to any cook's library.

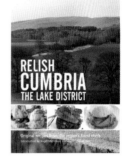

Relish North East

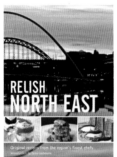

From the bustling city life in Newcastle, to the multitude of sleepy, rural villages, the North East has something for everyone.
An introduction from the North East's best known chef, Terry Laybourne, kicks off this culinary adventure through a rich and diverse region, with many varied recipes for you to try at home including a selection from the North East's two Masterchef finalists, John Calton and David Coulson, plus many others from award-winning chefs across the region.

LOOKING TO DINE IN THE UK'S FINEST RESTAURANTS?

Simply log on to relishpublications.co.uk and find the very best your region has to offer.

The Relish team has worked with all of the restaurants and chefs listed on the Relish website and have visited every highly recommended and acclaimed restaurant. These ingredients make the **Relish Restaurant Guide** genuine and unique.

If you would like to be taken on an epic journey to the finest restaurants in each region, download more mouth-watering recipes, or add to your collection of Relish books, visit **www.relishpublications.co.uk**

AL DENTE
Al dente describes vegetables that are cooked to the 'tender crisp' phase - still offering resistance to the bite, but cooked through. Al dente can also describe cooked pasta which is firm but not hard.

BAIN-MARIE
A pan or other container of hot water with a bowl placed on top of it. This allows the steam from the water to heat the bowl so ingredients can be gently heated or melted in the bowl.

BLANCH
Boiling an ingredient before removing it and plunging it in ice cold water in order to stop the cooking process.

BLIND BAKE
A method of baking that uses ceramic 'beans' to weigh down a pastry crust in order to cook it without a filling. One of our chefs suggest that coins may be used instead of beans since they conduct the heat well.

CLARIFIED BUTTER
Milk fat rendered from butter to separate the milk solids and water from the butterfat.

CONCASSE
To rough chop any ingredient, usually vegetables, most specifically applied to tomatoes, with tomato concasse being a tomato that has been peeled and seeded (seeds and skins removed).

CONFIT
A method of cooking where the meat is cooked submerged in a liquid to add flavour. Often this liquid is rendered fat.

DEGLAZE
A fancy term for using the flavour-packed brown bits stuck to the bottom of a pan to make a pan sauce or gravy.

EMULSION/EMULSIFIED
A mixture of two or more liquids that are normally immiscible (non mixable or unblendable). The combination of butter and water creates an emulsion.

JULIENNE
A culinary knife cut in which the food item is cut into long thin strips, similar to matchsticks.

JUS
The natural juices given off by the food. To prepare a natural jus, the cook may simply skim off the fat from the juices left after cooking and bring the remaining meat stock and water to a boil.

LIQUOR
The liquid that is left over from cooking of meat or vegetables. Can be incorporated into sauces and gravy.

MALTODEXTRIN
A food additive commonly used for the production of sodas and candy. It can also be found as an ingredient in a variety of other processed foods.

MONTE
Sauce finishing. Adding small quantities of butter (emulsify) to thicken a sauce

PANE
To coat with flour, beaten egg and breadcrumbs.

PATE A BOMBE
French term for a mixture used as a base for making chocolate mousse and other mousse-like desserts.

SEAL
To cook meat at a high temperature for a short period of time, resulting in a cooked crust on the outside and raw meat on the inside.

SOUS VIDE
Sous vide is French for 'under vacuum'. In culinary terms, sous vide is a cooking method in which food is vacuum sealed then immersed in a water bath and cooked at a very precise and consistent temperature.

TRIMOLENE
Used in the baking and confectionery industry to prevent recrystallisation of sugars. Will also enhance texture and smoothness to fillings, ice cream and ganache.

TUILE
A wafer thin biscuit that can be made of a variety of things. Often served to decorate a dish.

VAC PACK (VACUUM PACKING)
Vacuum packaging also allows for a special cooking method, sous vide.